The Radio Rentals Book of the
WORLD CUP '78

Kenny Dalglish of Scotland

The Radio Rentals Book of the

WORLD CUP '78

John Morgan and David Emery

A WOODHEAD-FAULKNER PUBLICATION

Published in association with Radio Rentals Limited by
Woodhead-Faulkner Limited, 8 Market Passage, Cambridge
CB2 3PF

© John Morgan and David Emery 1978

ISBN 0 85941 087 0

Design by Ken Vail

Production services by Book Production Consultants

Typesetting by Best Typesetting Limited, London

Printed in Great Britain by Lowe & Brydone Printers Limited,
Thetford, Norfolk

Foreword

by Ally MacLeod
Manager of Scotland

On June 1, Scotland will embark on what I believe could be the greatest football occasion in our history.

A few thousand Scots who will arrive by boat, plane, car and even submarine in Argentina will be privileged to have ringside seats. For those millions of others,

books like this serve as a wonderful guide to all the action on television and in the newspapers.

"Ally MacLeod's Tartan Army" is how the media are describing my team – and our followers. In some ways they are more right than they know. Because if we are to win this World Cup – which is within our capabilities – we will need to show the kind of discipline and single-mindedness they favour so much in military circles.

Too often in the past Scotland's great international efforts have been dissipated by off-field pressures. We must ensure it does not happen this time. But that's not to say we will in any way check our natural instincts of playing expressive soccer.

Win, lose or draw we will give the South Americans something to remember us by. How can we do otherwise with the squad of players I can call upon?

Hold on tight to your armchairs – we intend to make you sit up in them.

Ally MacLeod

The Authors

John Morgan, Chief Sports Writer of the *Daily Express*, is one of the most experienced sports journalists in Fleet Street. For 12 years he was Sports Editor of the *Express* before moving over to full-time writing and winning the Sports Writer of the Year award in 1972.

David Emery joined the *Daily Mail* at the age of 23 in 1970 and moved to the *Express* two years later. He served as a football correspondent before becoming Sports Features Editor.

Acknowledgements

The photographs on the following pages have been reproduced by kind permission of:

Associated Press: 43, 84, 90, 93, 104, 106
Beaverbrook Newspapers Ltd: 7, 38, 45, 51, 58, 67, 79, 109
Bob Thomas: 2, 5, 49, 98, 99
Colorsport: front cover, 55, 62, 72, 75, 86, 95, 101
Eammon McCabe Photosport: 82
Keystone Press Agency Ltd: 10, 14, 17, 20, 26, 29, 32, 115
Press Association: 36, 40, 88
SIGLA: 70

Contents

World Cup winners 1974: Gerd Müller of West Germany holds aloft the trophy accompanied by team-mate Wolfgang Overath. Who will follow them in 1978?

The World Cup 1930-1974

Uruguay 1930

Apart from the absence of England, the first World Cup set one other unfortunate precedent. It began with a scandal.

Bobby Moore and the bracelet incident in Bogota in 1970 and the reports of drunken Scottish players in Munich in 1974 were all in the future as Uruguay's lionised goalkeeper, Mazzali, crept into his team's hotel hours after curfew, shoes in hand, and was promptly sent home in disgrace.

Thirteen nations took part in the competition, which kicked off on July 13 – not, perhaps, a tournament for the superstitious. Certainly, the gremlins were working overtime to foil the much-vaunted opening of the new Uruguayan Centenary Stadium: heavy rain delayed its completion until the championships were well under way.

France, in commemoration of Bastille Day (July 14), played the first match and beat those perennial losers Mexico 4–1, despite their goalkeeper Alex Thepot being carried off with concussion after only ten minutes. It was one of the few successes to be recorded by European teams.

The four teams seeded at the head of the four groups were all from the Americas – including the United States, who were currently undergoing one of their periodic attempts to set the game up as a serious rival to gridiron. Indeed, as now, British players, especially Scots, were induced to try their luck in the States. One prime import was Alex Jackson, who discovered the land of opportunity was not, in fact, bursting with football fervour, and eventually returned to Scotland.

In Uruguay, the United States headed Group Four, Argentina led Group One, Brazil Group Two and Uruguay themselves Group Three.

In Group One it was the France–Argentina match which proved the key encounter, and the most controversial. The Argentinians had a superb team, who had finished as runners-up to Uruguay in the Olympic final two years earlier in Amsterdam. The star of that side, left-winger Raimondo Orsi, had been transferred to Juventus of Italy. But enough great players remained, including the awesome centre-half Luisito Monti, who was himself later sold to Juventus and with Orsi was destined to win a World Cup winners' medal playing for Italy in 1934.

Four years earlier in Uruguay Monti was to focus his full menacing attention on the brilliant Frenchman Marcel Pinel, the lynch-pin and dangerman of the French strategy. Pinel reported later that Monti kicked him every time he went near him, beginning the Argentinian reputation for ruthlessness that has followed them ever since and culminated in England manager Sir Alf Ramsey labelling them "animals" during the 1966 Finals.

It was Monti who scored the decisive goal after 81 minutes, sending a free kick past the unsighted Thepot. Then came pandemonium. With six minutes of time remaining the Brazilian referee, Rego, whistled the end of the game. The Argentinian fans stormed over the safety barriers and the French crowded around Rego in dismay. After hurried, heated discussions among officials the game was restarted and the six minutes completed. But the score remained the same.

The French captain who had led the complaints about the early whistle, right-half Alex Villaplane, was later to be shot for collaboration with the Germans during the Second World War.

Like the Argentinians, the Rumanians also won their first game – a blood-curdling 3–1 triumph over the ruthless Peruvians. Rumania's left-back Steiner had his leg broken in one incident and Peru's captain, De Las Casas, was sent off. But it was to prove a fruitless victory. Rumania were thrashed 4–0 by Uruguay, who also accounted for Peru 1–0 to move into the semi-finals with a 100 per cent record.

The United States, trained on Anglo-Saxon principles of speed and stamina and containing six expatriate British professionals, booked themselves a semi-final place against Argentina with identical 3–0 defeats of Belgium and Paraguay.

It was left to Yugoslavia to carry the flag for Europe. They crushed Bolivia 4–0 and trimmed the emergent Brazilians 2–1 to line up against their Uruguayan hosts in the last four.

Yugoslavia were in front within four minutes of the start of that semi-final. The 80,000 spectators were stunned. Surely this could not be happening to the Olympic champions and tournament favourites? No, it couldn't. The Yugoslavs collapsed in the second half and Pedro Cea scored a hat-trick as Uruguay went on to win 6–1.

The score was the same in the other semi-final, in favour of Argentina. The United States, although pre-match favourites, had no answer to the Latin skills of their opponents. If they had any doubts that it was not their day, they were answered early in the match. The team's medical attendant ran on to the field to protest about one refereeing decision, threw down his box in disgust, accidentally smashed a bottle of chloroform and was rendered unconscious.

The stadium at Montevideo was packed with 90,000 spectators for the Uruguay–Argentina final. In the days before the game an armada of boats set off across the River Plate from Buenos Aires carrying Argentinian fans.

All were searched for guns before the game began. The referee, Belgium's Jean Langenus, was in fear of his life and the teams were under 24-hour guard. But in the end the match was a serene advert for world football, with Uruguay deservedly winning 4–2.

The Uruguayan team pictured before the 1930 final: they went on to beat Argentina 4–2

Right-winger Pablo Dorado gave them a twelfth-minute lead, but in the thirty-fifth minute Carlos Peucelle equalised and then Argentina took the lead through Stabile. The River Plate brigade were ecstatic. Ten minutes after half-time they were silenced as Cea ran through to level the score and sow the seeds of doubt in Argentinian minds. As Uruguay maintained their fierce pressure even the indestructible Monti began to wilt and Santos Iriarte and centre-forward Castro ran past him to score the decisive goals. While the British lion slept, Uruguay had conquered the world.

Italy 1934

Uruguay, annoyed by the manner in which the majority of Europe had snubbed them four years earlier and embroiled in a players' strike, refused to send a team to the second World Cup. Otherwise, the 1934 competition was a far more representative affair.

Italy was rife with Mussolini's Fascism and, as in Berlin during the Olympic Games two years later, the arena of sport was transformed into a propaganda vehicle. In every Italian newspaper the strutting dictator, Il Duce, was pictured posing proudly with his team of élite young athletes.

Italy were one of two obviously outstanding teams in the tournament. The other was Austria. Both were founded on British principles. The Italians were managed by Vittorio Pozzo, a passionate, mercurial man who enjoyed an almost Freudian understanding of the human mind. Motivation was an unknown word then, but Pozzo, brilliant at gauging the way to draw the best from his men, might have invented it. As a student in England he had watched and learned from the great Manchester United team of 1908. Now his Italian team combined British aggression and strong, surging attack with the subtle ball artistry of Giuseppe Meazza and the former Argentinian star, left-winger Raimondo Orsi.

Austria had been christened the "*Wunderbar* team" in the early 1930s. They were coached by a little Lancastrian, Jimmy Hogan, who had been one of the first British soccer missionaries to spread the word in Europe. Like Pozzo, Hogan recognised the importance of blending British-style fitness to Continental-style finesse. In 1932 Hogan's team had given mighty England the fright of their lives before losing 4–3 at Stamford Bridge in a desperately tight finish.

Italy, though, as hosts were favourites for the tournament, which attracted an original entry of 29. Of the 16 finalists, 12 came from Europe.

With Uruguay petulantly sitting it out, the depleted South American challenge was headed by Argentina, although even they insisted on leaving many of their leading players at home for fear they would be poached by the Italians, as centre-half Luisito Monti had been in

1930. Monti was now the key figure in the Italian team. The system of four qualifying groups, as practised four years earlier in Uruguay, was scrapped and replaced by a sudden-death knock-out competition. It was highly unsatisfactory, and meant that first-round losers like the United States, Argentina and Brazil had spent weeks travelling half-way round the world for just one game.

The Italians opened the tournament in Rome, watched by Mussolini, and despatched a weak United States team 7–1, with a hat-trick from Schiavio. Brazil tumbled 3–1 to the fine Spanish side and Argentina fell 3–2 to Sweden. Austria, surprisingly, had a tough time of it against France in Turin before finally edging home 3–2 with a blatantly offside goal. That earned Austria a quarter-final pairing with Hungary, another team influenced by Jimmy Hogan. But the promised clash of skills quickly deteriorated into a savage brawl before the Hungarian winger Markos was sent off and Austria went on doggedly to a 2–0 victory.

But if Austria collected a few bruises, this stage of the competition proved almost fatal to the Italians. They were pitted against Spain and the legendary Zamora. This veteran goalkeeper was a hero in his country after a series of breathtaking displays and, to the Italians' misery, the quarter-final continued the sequence. Spain took the lead in the first half and Italy managed to scramble a desperate equaliser only because Zamora was impeded. Zamora, who had been buffeted throughout, was unfit for the replay the next day which the Italians squeezed through by the only goal. In each game the referee's leniency towards the Italians was criticised. The officials, observers believed, were being intimidated by the fierce nationalism of the crowds.

So to the semi-finals – the *Wunderbar* Austrians versus Mussolini's Italians. The nation waited – but the rain didn't. Down it poured in Milan where the game was to be staged, turning the pitch into a heavy, clinging surface which was totally unsuited to the Austrians' short passing game. They went out by the only goal of the match, scored by Guaita, the Italian right-winger.

Italian manager Vittorio Pozzo *(left)* gives his players a pep-talk before the start of extra time in the 1934 final. Captain and goalkeeper Combi *(centre)* looks apprehensive

Czechoslovakia, meantime, had progressed to the other semi-final by defeating Rumania 2–1 and Switzerland 3–2. Now they proved far too mobile for the Germans and a 3–1 victory booked them a confrontation with Italy in the final.

For 70 minutes the 55,000 crowd packing the Rome stadium waited for the first goal and then the Czech left-winger Puc capitalised on a period of intense pressure to smash the ball home. Eight minutes from the end Italy equalised as Orsi ran through, dummied to shoot with his left foot, hit the ball instead with his right and watched as it curled over goalkeeper Planicka and into the net. The following day Orsi was to try the same manoeuvre 20 times in front of an empty net – and fail to score each time.

In extra time the superior fitness of the Italians took its toll on the tiring Czechs and after seven minutes Schiavio completed a passing movement between Meazza and Guaita to score the goal which allowed a beaming Mussolini to bestow the Jules Rimet trophy upon his own captain, Combi.

France 1938

The shadow of war hung black and heavy over Europe by the time of the third World Cup. The Nazis had already occupied Austria, disbanding their *Wunderbar* team and co-opting several players into the German side managed by Sepp Herberger. Spain was ravaged by civil war and Great Britain was still at odds with FIFA.

Uruguay, still fuming over their cold reception by Europe in 1930, again decided not to come and the Argentinians, piqued that their request to stage the tournament had been turned down, stayed away in a huff. Of the magical South Americans, only Brazil made the long haul to France. And they were destined to meet their match in the team everyone had to beat – the reigning World Champions, Italy.

Vittorio Pozzo was still the manager but the nature of his side had changed dramatically in the intervening four years. No longer were Italy the aggressive, physical side that the world had witnessed winning the trophy on their home soil. Now, with only two survivors from the 1934 team, Peppino Meazza and Giovanni Ferrari, they placed the emphasis on skill. Their confidence was high, with Pozzo secretly predicting that nothing could prevent a second triumph if they played to form. It was a prediction which came tantalisingly close to grief in the very first match, against little Norway. As in 1934 the tournament was organised on a knockout basis, and the exit sign was beckoning Italy a couple of times before they eventually squeezed home 2–1 in extra time, Norway having been denied victory when Brustad's goal was declared offside.

The shock of the round was the defeat of Hitler's Germany. The Master Race crashed 4–2 to the humble Swiss after drawing their first encounter 1–1, and to make matters worse Switzerland played much of the game with only ten men.

Poland, making their first appearance in the competition, went out 6–5 to Brazil in a breathtaking orgy of attacking football – and then sent their conquerors a good-luck telegram for the next round. Other newcomers Cuba proved to know far more about the game than they had any right to and knocked out Rumania 2–1, after previously drawing with them 3–3. The effort, however, drained the excitable Cubans both physically and mentally and they plummeted in the next round, beaten 8–0 by the rampant Swedes.

France, meantime, had accounted for neighbours Belgium 3–1 to keep alive hopes that the host country could prevail for the third time running. But the dream died in front of 58,000 in Paris at the hands of Italy and their centre-forward Silvio Piola in particular. Piola, a tall, god-like figure who was to play his last international as late as 1952, scored twice in the second half after France had gone in at the interval all square at 1–1.

In Bordeaux, at the newly built municipal stadium, Czechoslovakia and Brazil kicked lumps out of each other in the most brutal match the World Cup had seen. Two Brazilians and a Czech were sent off and two Czechs were badly injured, one breaking an arm, the other a leg. The match floundered in a sea of blood and bruises to a 2–2 draw. In an amazingly docile replay, Brazil, with nine changes, triumphed 2–1.

The semi-final brought the match of the competition – Brazil *v.* Italy. Yet one man who did not seem to recognise its significance was the Brazilian manager Pimenta. Astoundingly, he decided to leave out Brazil's star forwards Leonidas and Tim, telling a disbelieving world: "I am saving them for the final." Whether it was sheer bravado or a tactical ploy has never become clear, but it probably cost Brazil their first appearance in a World Cup final. In the event they quickly went a goal down, lost a second from the penalty spot and went out 2–1.

The start of the 1938 final: Italian captain Meazza *(left)* shakes hands with Hungary's Sarosi, watched by French referee Capdeville

Hungary, who had beaten the weak Dutch East Indies 6–0 and Switzerland 2–0, proved far too strong for the Swedes and won 5–1, despite conceding a goal after just 35 seconds. As if in evidence of their superiority a blackbird quietly hopped around their half for much of the latter stages.

The final proved an anti-climax, although many had half-suspected it would and stayed away from the giant stadium at Colombes in Paris. Only 45,000 turned out to see Italy tackle Hungary and they were inadequately rewarded with a mediocre match. Italy took the lead after six minutes through Colaussi. Hungary equalised immediately but by half time Italy were 3–1 up and always in control against the ponderous Hungarians. They went on to win 4–2 and take the trophy for the second successive time. It was to be the last World Cup competition for 12 years. The dogs of war were out and running.

Brazil 1950

The fourth World Cup marked England's entry into the competition – and her greatest humiliation. The nightmare which had been stalking the Football Association ever since its blinkered, insular attitude had cut it off from the realities of world soccer finally pounced in the mountain air of Belo Horizonte. There, the cream of England – players like Tom Finney, Stanley Mortensen, Wilf Mannion, Billy Wright and right-back Alf Ramsey – were beaten 1–0 by the United States, a miscellaneous collection of Yanks plus a Haitian centre-forward, a Belgian left-back and a Scottish captain called Eddie McIlvenny who had been given a free transfer from Wrexham, then luxuriating in the Third Division North. It was the day the mighty did not simply fall; rather they crashed to earth with the thunderous roar of an Alpine avalanche. And in the beginning it had seemed so safe and straightforward for England . . .

At the end of the Second World War, rejoicing in the climate of co-operation and affection between the Allies, Britain had deigned to return to FIFA and were duly invited to take part in the 1950 World Cup. The Home

International Championship was to serve as the qualifying group and the top two countries would be eligible for the World Cup Finals in Brazil. England duly won, with Scotland as runners-up. The Scots, with blind pride, declined to compete as also-rans to England. They were one among a plethora of withdrawals. France pulled out because the match venues were too far apart, Austria decided their team was too young, Russia and Hungary were maintaining splendid isolation, Czechoslovakia fell out with the World Cup committee and Germany were excluded anyway.

The reigning World Champions, Italy, had been torn asunder by the appalling Superga air crash in May 1949 when 17 Torino players, most of them internationals, had died on a hillside outside Turin. Manager Vittorio Pozzo had gone as well, sacked the previous year. England, entering the arena like the white knight, had only to fear the fast-developing Brazilians, and surely even they would be no match for the country who had given the game to the world and were invincible at home?

The tournament system had been changed from that of 1934 and 1938. Now it would operate on a group basis throughout – the winners of four qualifying groups going through to a final pool which again was played on a league basis. Sudden death had suddenly died.

England started well enough, beating Chile 2–0 in Rio with goals from Mortensen and Mannion, and then travelled out to Belo Horizonte for the formality of playing the United States. Even the Americans' coach gave them no chance and many of the players stayed up half the night on the eve of the match. England, expected to win by a rugby score, began as if they would. Time after time the American defence was ripped apart only for the final effort to travel agonisingly wide or be miraculously saved. Still England didn't worry – the goals would come. Then, after 37 minutes, the roof fell in. Behr, the American left-half, crossed, Haitian centre-forward Larry Gaetjens got his head to the ball and it sailed past goalkeeper Bert Williams and into the net. A header from Jimmy Mullen seemed to have crossed the United States' goal-line in the second half but the referee thought otherwise. England, the unbeatable, had been beaten 1–0 by a joke team.

Even the newspapers refused to believe it. One assumed a mistake had been made in the wire room and printed the score as 10–1 to England. It meant that England had to beat Spain in their last game in Rio to stay in the World Cup. They didn't. Despite the recall of Stanley Matthews, the defeat in Belo Horizonte had shattered morale and England went down by the only goal of the game, although Jackie Milburn had what looked a perfectly good equaliser disallowed.

Meanwhile, Brazil, Sweden and Uruguay had battled through to join Spain in the final pool. Brazil showed just how far England had lagged behind in world standards by beating Spain 6–1. They also put seven goals past Sweden to go into the final match against Uruguay needing only a draw to become World Champions. Uruguay, who had drawn 2–2 with Spain and beaten Sweden 3–2 rather luckily, were mainly a young side with a strategy built around their strong, attacking centre-half, Obdulio Varela. On paper, Brazil were clear favourites. Yet they were not confident . . . Uruguay had long been their bogey team.

Brazil, sparkling and inventive in front of the 200,000 at the Maracana Stadium, Rio, dominated the first half. Only a series of superb saves from Maspoli and desperate defensive work kept Uruguay in with a chance. Brazil went ahead through Friaca but Uruguay equalised through Schiaffino and then, 11 minutes from the end, Ghiggia scored Uruguay's winner.

In two attempts, spanning 20 years, Uruguay had won the World Cup twice. In the next 20, they would reach the semi-finals twice and be defeated both times.

Switzerland 1954

If previous World Cups had been won by men scoring goals, then the 1954 tournament in Switzerland was surely won by one man kicking another. The culprit was West Germany's centre-half Werner Liebrich; the victim Hungary's brilliant inside-forward Ferenc Puskas.

The Hungarians, the most gifted side of their era, had sailed in to Switzerland on a sea of goals. In six sensational months they had put 13 past England – laying England's "invincible" myth once and for all at Wembley on November 25, 1953, with a 6–3 demolition and then totally humiliating them 7–1 in Budapest the following May.

The Hungarians – the Magical Magyars, as Fleet Street had dubbed them – were a team of wondermen. The incomparable Puskas with the left foot as lethal as a sword thrust; the deep-lying centre-forward Nandor Hidegkuti, the deadly Sandor Kocsis and the flying goalkeeper Gyula Grosics. There seemed nothing to stop them collecting the Jules Rimet trophy. Certainly not England, who were still dazed by the magnitude of their twin defeats, or Scotland, who had decided to enter the competition for the first time.

The formula of the tournament was changed yet again. The 16 qualifying nations were divided into four groups, but each team played only two games instead of three. Two teams in each group were seeded and did not play one another – a highly criticised development. If two teams finished level on points for second place in a group they would play off for a place in the quarter-finals. From the quarter-finals onwards the competition became sudden death.

The early games brought an avalanche of goals. Uruguay put seven past Scotland without reply, Hungary put nine past the bewildered South Koreans and Austria hammered Czechoslovakia 5–0. For Scotland it was a humiliating end to an uncomfortable trip. They were racked by internal strife among the officials, lost their other game to Austria 1–0 and returned home pointless and petulant.

It was in the other high-scoring massacre of the qualifying rounds that the World Cup was surely won and lost. Hungary, with Kocsis scoring four, destroyed West Germany 8–3, but in the course of the game Puskas was kicked on the leg by Liebrich – an injury which was to play a decisive role in the final the following week.

England proceeded to the last eight by winning Group Four with a 4–4 draw against Belgium and a 2–0 victory over Switzerland. They were joined by Brazil, Yugoslavia, West Germany, Uruguay, Austria, Italy and Hungary.

It was this stage of the competition which produced the infamous Battle of Berne – the match between Hungary and Brazil where superb players lost their heads both on and off the field. Brazil had an outstanding team, which included the young Didi, making his first World Cup appearance, Nilton Santos and Djalma Santos at full-back and a fast, raiding winger called Julinho. Even against Hungary their skill could have proved decisive. But they never waited to find out.

Hidegkuti scored first – and had his shorts ripped off. Kocsis headed a second and then Brazil scored from the spot. By half-time the game was out of control. Hungary scored a penalty, Julinho made it 3–2 and then all hell broke loose. Nilton Santos and Boszik had a fight in the middle of the field and were sent off by British referee Arthur Ellis. Humberto Tozzi, the Brazilian inside-left, was sent off for kicking, and Djalma Santos chased a Hungarian across the field. Hungary finally won 4–2. But the match was not yet over as far as the Brazilians were concerned.

They turned out the lights in the dressing-room tunnel and lay in wait for the Hungarians. Then they invaded the dressing-room and set about them. The fierce free-for-all lasted several minutes before stewards and officials prised the warring factions apart. Brazil travelled home in disgrace.

England's interest was ended in Basle, where indifferent goalkeeping by Gil Merrick let Uruguay through for a 4–2 victory, despite fine performances from England's twin wizards of the dribble Stanley Matthews and Tom Finney and the bludgeoning forward play of Nat Lofthouse.

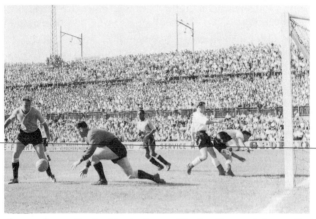

A goal-mouth incident from England's match against Uruguay in the 1954 tournament

The semi-finals provided Uruguay's first-ever World Cup defeat – 4–2 at the hands of Hungary in what is recognised as one of the finest matches of all time. Hungary led 2–0 but injury-stricken Uruguay hauled themselves back to 2–2 before gallantly losing in extra time.

In the final Hungary would meet West Germany, who had beaten Yugoslavia 2–0 in the quarter-finals and a disappointing Austria 6–1 in the semis. What could possibly go wrong for Hungary? Hadn't they crushed the Germans 8–3 only a few days earlier?

Well, for a start, Puskas insisted on playing, having missed the previous two matches with his leg injury. He was still far from fit but he was a powerful, respected voice in the Hungarian camp. It seemed a happy decision as Hungary stormed to a 2–0 lead in eight minutes before the 55,000 crowd at Berne. Puskas himself scored the first and Czibor the second. But the Germans sensationally fought back to equalise and then began to gain control as Puskas, obviously labouring, missed chances. A German centre was only partially cleared and Rahn shot them ahead. Five minutes from time Puskas at last raced clear and drove the ball home. But Welsh linesman Mervyn Griffiths had his flag raised for offside. As Holland were to find in 1974, the better team had come second.

Sweden 1958

For the first and only time all four of the home countries qualified for the World Cup Finals and, indeed, England might well have won it but for the tragic Manchester United air crash at Munich which robbed them of Roger Byrne, Tommy Taylor and the peerless Duncan Edwards. The Hungarians, too, had been ravaged. The revolution had cost them dear, although Hidegkuti, Grosics and Bozsik survived from the 1954 immortals.

Waiting in the wings, though, was a new World Cup star, a wondrous young player from Brazil: Pele, the black pearl. Then only 17, he was to stamp his class on this tournament of talents and illuminate a Brazilian team playing exciting 4–2–4 football with the likes of Didi, Garrincha and Vava.

England, captained by Billy Wright and inspired by Johnny Haynes, decided they could do without Matthews, Lofthouse and the young Bobby Charlton. They were to discover otherwise. Their first match, against Russia in Gothenburg, ended in a 2–2 draw, although the most significant statistic was the injury which ruled Tom Finney out of the rest of the competition.

England had been pitted against Brazil in the qualifying

groups and their eventual match provided Billy Wright's men with their finest hour-and-a-half of World Cup action so far. With England, in fact, looking the better side, it was the only match of the tournament in which Brazil failed to score. The goalless draw meant that England had to play off against Russia for a place in the quarter-finals. They created chances, hit a post, but eventually fell to the only goal when goalkeeper Colin McDonald sent a throw directly to a Russian player.

Scotland, too, went out at the qualifying group stage, losing to France 2–1 – on Dave Mackay's debut – and drawing 1–1 with Yugoslavia. Wales, though, with the magnificent John Charles released from Juventus to play for them, beat Hungary 2–1 in the Group Three play-off, and Northern Ireland, captained by Danny Blanchflower, beat Czechoslovakia 2–1 in the Group One play-off, both goals coming from winger Peter McParland. So, of the four home countries, two were through to the last eight – the unfancied ones, perhaps, but they were through. Alas, they were to progress no further.

Northern Ireland, tottering under an increasing burden of injuries, finally ran out of steam and into a French team rejoicing in the partnership of Raymond Kopa and Just Fontaine. They lost 4–0, Fontaine scoring twice. In Gothenburg, Wales produced a magnificent display before losing 1–0 to Brazil and a Pele goal. John Charles was ruled out through injury but with his brother Mel Charles dominant in the air and Jack Kelsey superb in goal, they were a match for the Brazilians' scintillating samba rhythm. Pele's late goal came, in fact, from a deflection off Stuart Williams and it is a measure of the fright Wales gave Brazil that Pele was later to describe it as the most important of his career.

On to the semi-finals: Brazil *v.* France and Sweden, the hosts, *v.* West Germany. George Raynor, the Yorkshireman who coached the Swedes, had forecast they would reach the final long before the competition started. And so it proved – although the Germans, led by the emergent Uwe Seeler, contributed heavily to their own 3–1 defeat. With the score at 1–1 and Germany in control Juskowiak was sent off for a foolish kick – and the balance swung firmly in Sweden's favour.

Stockholm 1958: Pele, in his first World Cup final, challenges Swedish goalkeeper Svensson

A hat-trick by Pele gave Brazil a crushing 5–2 victory over France and a place in the final against Sweden at Stockholm in front of 50,000 strangely muted Swedes. Raynor, who had been right all along so far, finally made his first mistake. The Brazilians, he forecast, would panic if they fell a goal behind. Score the first goal and Sweden would win the World Cup.

Liedholm did just that after only four minutes, but Brazil kept their heads admirably. Two runs by Garrincha making two goals for Vava gave Brazil a 2–1 lead at half-time. Then they really began to play. The full creative kaleidoscope of Brazilian football was given reign on the most appropriate of stages. Pele scored two sublime goals – including one astonishing effort where he took the ball on his instep with his back to goal, chipped it over his head, turned and drove it on the volley into the corner of the net. Zagalo scored the other, with Simonsson catching Brazil on the break to add Sweden's consolatory second. The 5–2 scoreline remains the largest in a World Cup final. The Brazilians had arrived, and they meant to stay.

Chile 1962

Where Sweden had provided a breathtaking competition with a veritable cavalcade of goals and exciting, attacking play, Chile staged the most boring of all the World Cup Finals. Negative, defensive football was the order of the day and even the extravagant Brazilians could never quite conjure up the magic of four years earlier after losing Pele through injury in their opening game.

Only England of the home countries managed to qualify this time and they were plunged into a group containing Argentina, Hungary and Bulgaria. The young Bobby Moore had just entered the England team but even he provided scant evidence of the glory that was to come his way in England's drab opening match – a 2–1 defeat by Hungary. England perked up against Argentina in their next game, winning 3–1 with goals from Ron Flowers, Bobby Charlton and Jimmy Greaves, and then ensured a place in the quarter-finals with a crushingly featureless 0–0 draw with Bulgaria.

Over at Vina del Mar the now aging Brazilians had their problems. Their group included Spain – managed by the masterly Helenio Herrera and boasting the refugee Hungarian, Puskas, and the legendary Di Stefano in their squad – and a Czech team revolving around the artistry of Josef Masopust.

Brazil beat Mexico 2–0 in their opening game and then lost Pele with a thigh strain. Their remodelled team, including Vava and Didi in midfield, drew 0–0 with the Czechs and then came the promised thriller with the improving Spaniards. Herrera named a youthful team, aiming to smother the Brazilian brilliance with effort and strong running. It paid dividends as Spain took the lead, but then Garrincha made two goals for Pele's understudy Amarildo to settle the contest.

England were to provide the next victims in the Brazilian march to the final. Gerry Hitchens, the centre-forward Aston Villa had sold to Inter-Milan, kept England in the game with an equaliser in the first half, but Ron Springett's vulnerability to long shots was demonstrated all too vividly when he was twice beaten and the Brazilians swept through 3–1.

In the semi-finals Brazil would meet their hosts Chile, whose path through the tournament had been strewn with controversy. To qualify from their group they had needed to beat Italy in Santiago. They succeeded, 2–0, but not before two Italians had been sent off by British referee Ken Aston and Chile's Leonel Sanchez had, un-detected, broken Maschio's nose with a left hook. Despite the wild street parties and fervently partisan demonstrations which had accompanied their progress, Chile proved no match for the Brazilians. Garrincha, in irrepressible form, took them apart, scoring twice in the 4–2 victory.

Czechoslovakia, who had quietly qualified behind Russia in Group Three, continued their demure progress to the final by beating Yugoslavia 3–1 in front of only

5,000 spectators at Vina del Mar. Everyone had eyes only for the Brazil–Chile match.

The Czechs had struck their form at the right moment and some experts were even tipping them for a shock win in the final, where they looked to be on to a good thing when Masopust stroked a fine goal in the early stages. Instead the game was to change dramatically after two dreadful goalkeeping errors by Schroiff. First he let Amarildo's shot squeeze past him, then he dropped a high lob for Vava to score. Brazil eventually won 3–1, the first country since Italy to capture successive World Cups. Could they achieve the hat-trick?

An ugly incident from the 1962 tournament: team-mates come to the aid of Italy's Maschio after he has been felled by opponent Sanchez in the match with Chile

England 1966

Jack Charlton sank to the Wembley turf and wept, Nobby Stiles grinned gap-toothed in amazed delight and Alf Ramsey, the man who had achieved the miracle, the manager who had finally led England to the World Cup, sat solemn and thoughtful on the trainer's bench, savouring the moment in his mind with no outward show of emotion.

Ramsey, the former Spurs and England full-back, the professional's professional who had led little Ipswich Town from the Third Division to the League Championship, had fulfilled his promise. As he had predicted to a disbelieving public a full three years earlier, England had won the World Cup. And they had won it in style.

Ramsey's cold acceptance of soccer's greatest prize surprised the nation, but it was totally expected by the men who knew him best – his players. Throughout his reign as England manager, Ramsey had little time for anyone connected with English football apart from his players. They responded to this attitude with a fierce loyalty, forging for the first time a true team spirit and an understanding of collective responsibility.

As at Ipswich, Ramsey set his stall out in the most practical terms – making the best of what talent was available rather than deciding upon a system of play and then moulding men around it. To begin with, he persevered with England's traditional strength – wingers. But finding no one sufficiently skilful to follow in the illustrious steps of Matthews and Finney, he elected for a more workmanlike 4–3–3 system with a withdrawn winger playing in midfield. The "Wingless Wonders", as they became known, baffled the world with this hitherto unknown formation.

It had first been used with devastating effect against Spain six months before the World Cup Finals in England. With Bobby Charlton dropping deeper than an orthodox attacker and becoming, in effect, an extra midfield man, England won 2–0, and won looking good. Ramsey's mind was made up – this was the way to win the World Cup.

With Charlton in midfield, Bobby Moore in defence and Gordon Banks in goal, Ramsey possessed three truly world-class players. Around them he blended the pace and aggressive tackling of full-backs George Cohen and Ray Wilson, the aerial ability of big Jack Charlton, the non-stop action of young Alan Ball and the competitive will of Nobby Stiles. Others gradually asserted their claims – the selfless Roger Hunt up front and the subtle Martin Peters in midfield. Only one place truly remained contested – the striking role filled by the genius of Jimmy Greaves. Eventually Ramsey was to reveal his innermost philosophy by discarding Greaves with the final in sight and selecting the more straightforward, reliable Geoff Hurst.

England's challenge, though, opened more with the echoing sound of a raspberry rather than a heroic roll of drums: a goalless draw with Uruguay at Wembley, boring and frustrating. A 2–0 victory over Mexico with goals from Bobby Charlton and Hunt gave cause for hope but then followed a shapeless 2–0 win over France – and controversy. Stiles, the bantamweight mascot of Ramsey's team, was severely criticised for over-robust tackling. Ramsey was urged to drop him by senior FA officials. He declined. The team was still very much his affair, and his alone. The point was taken.

If Stiles raised a few temperatures, then the international barometer was sent soaring in the quarter-finals as England were pitted against Argentina, struggling to regain a measure of their former glory. From the start it was all too clear that Argentina were content to gain a result by any means possible. They obstructed, ankle-tapped, kicked, spat at and irritated England wherever possible. A procession of names went into the notebook of the West German referee, who finally, almost at his wits' end, sent off the Argentinian captain Rattin for dissent. For eight long minutes Rattin refused to go as the crowd bayed their disapproval and the players hung around in groups, bewildered by events. Eventually he slunk away, leaving Hurst to win the game with a header 13 minutes from the end and Ramsey to label the Argentinians "animals".

In the other groups momentous events were in progress. The little North Koreans, captivating the crowd at Middlesbrough, knocked out the mighty Italians, and an aging Brazil, minus the injured Pele, fell 3–1 to Hungary and their first World Cup defeat for 12 years – in fact, their first since Hungary had beaten them in the infamous Battle of Berne.

In the semi-finals England were matched against the inventive, volatile Portuguese and their lethal striker Eusebio, who finished as leading marksman in the competition with nine goals. With Bobby Charlton in superb form England gave their finest display so far to win 2–1.

In the final they would meet West Germany, who had followed a 4–0 thrashing of Uruguay in the quarter-finals with a 2–1 defeat of Russia in the semis. The stage was set for a masterpiece.

At 3 p.m. on Saturday, July 30, the streets of England were deserted as the nation sat glued to their televisions. At 3.13 a collective wail rent the air as Germany went ahead through Haller. But not since 1938 had the team scoring first gone on to win . . . history was on Ramsey's side. Six minutes later Hurst headed in Moore's free kick: 1–1. A third West Ham man, Peters, cracked home a rebound after 78 minutes: 2–1. Nothing, it seemed, could prevent Moore climbing the steps of the Royal Box to collect the Jules Rimet trophy for England. Then, in the final seconds, Weber scrambled a heart-stopping equaliser.

As pulses beat fast and heavy throughout Wembley,

Ramsey remained cool. The Germans were tired, he argued, England's superb fitness and meticulous team training would prevail. In the final analysis, though, it was the individual performances of the red-haired little dynamo Alan Ball and the lion-hearted Geoff Hurst that won the day. Ball, galloping down the right with astonishing freshness, laid on a controversial third for Hurst. Had the ball crossed the goal-line when it thundered down from the bar? The referee decided it had.

Geoff Hurst's shot in the 1966 final that gave England their decisive third goal

3–2. Hurst rendered all arguments academic as he added a fourth for his historic hat-trick. England, at last, were back on top of the world. Could they stay there?

Mexico 1970

England had assembled a team arguably better even than their 1966 version by the time of the next World Cup. Roger Hunt had gone, to be replaced by the dynamic Francis Lee; Cohen and Wilson had given way to Keith Newton and Terry Cooper; Alan Mullery followed the combative Stiles; and Brian Labone had ousted Jack Charlton. Moore, Bobby Charlton and Banks remained – pillars of a formidable side.

Yet from such auspicious beginnings, England were to

be afflicted by a chain of misfortunes. Even before the tournament had started, Moore had been put under house arrest in Bogota on a trumped-up charge of stealing a bracelet. When he did finally rejoin the squad in Mexico City it was to find the locals incensed by Ramsey's aloof bearing and intent on reaping an insidious revenge: car horns blared and throngs of people chanted rowdily throughout the night below the windows of the England hotel, interrupting sleep and fraying tempers.

After one such night England, in Guadalajara, lost a thrilling match 1–0 to Brazil after Jeff Astle had missed an open-goal chance to equalise. It was an encouraging, if downbeat, beginning. But the optimism it engendered was justified as England beat both Czechoslovakia and Rumania 1–0 to progress untroubled into the quarter-finals and a meeting with their 1966 victims, West Germany.

Elsewhere the minnows struggled for a moment's glory like North Korea four years earlier – and failed. El Salvador, whose qualifying competition win over Honduras had sparked a bloody war and 3,000 deaths, failed to score a goal, while Morocco from Africa and Israel from Asia failed to win a game.

In Leon, as England prepared for their ill-fated meeting with the Germans, the misfortune which had dogged them from the start struck again. Banks was ruled out of the match with stomach trouble. It was a dreadful blow – Banks had been performing better than at any time in his career. One save from a Pele header in the match with Brazil had been described as the finest ever made. With Banks confined to bed, Peter Bonetti took over – and walked straight into a nightmare.

It all started so well. England, playing with the authority and poise of true World Champions, cruised into a two-goal lead. Ramsey, perhaps feeling victory was a formality, substituted Bobby Charlton and Martin Peters to rest them from the rigours of the heat and the altitude and save them for the next match. The result was traumatic. Franz Beckenbauer, released from his role as Charlton's policeman, began trundling forward in loping, defence-splitting runs. Suddenly Bonetti was late down on one of his long-range shots and Germany were back in the game.

Their manager, Helmut Schoen, showing greater understanding of the role of substitutes than Ramsey, brought on winger Grabowski to terrorise the right flank. But their equalising goal was engineered by pure luck, the ball bouncing off the back of Seeler's head and past Bonetti's outstretched hands. In extra time the explosive Müller completed the amazing transformation by volleying the winner. The game had been Charlton's 106th cap – a record. It also proved to be his last.

In Guadalajara the dynamic Brazilians routed Peru 4–2 in another quarter-final, with Tostao scoring twice and other goals coming from Rivelino and Jairzinho, who was to score in every round of the tournament. Italy, after a defensive start, blasted Mexico 4–1 in Toluca and Uruguay edged out Russia 1–0 in Mexico City.

The 1970 final has just ended and Brazil are World Champions for the third time: Pele is acclaimed by his fans

Germany's semi-final with Italy provided a riot of goals in extra time after full time had seen them locked at 1–1. An injury to Beckenbauer's shoulder proved a decisive handicap to the Germans, who went down 4–3. Goals by Jairzinho and Rivelino gave Brazil a 2–1 win over South American neighbours Uruguay and the other place in the final.

There, Italy once more adopted a defensive stance – and played into the hands of the extrovert Brazilians. Pele opened the scoring with a header, Boninsegna equalised, but then Gerson, Jairzinho and Carlos Alberto gave Brazil an easy 4–1 victory to claim the World Cup for the third time – and the Jules Rimet trophy outright.

West Germany 1974

As in Argentina this summer, Scotland were Britain's sole representatives in the World Cup Finals. England had fallen – by drawing with Wales and failing to beat a fine Polish side at Wembley. In the wake of the retributions Sir Alf Ramsey, the manager who had led England to their greatest triumph eight years earlier, was to be sacked. His record: played 113, won 69, drawn 27, lost 17. Northern Ireland, too, were forced to watch from afar, having lost a crucial match in Cyprus.

Under the new managership of Willie Ormond, the successor to Tommy Docherty, Scotland edged through to the Finals in West Germany at the expense of Czechoslovakia. Once there, though, all the old problems of temperament afflicting Scottish sides came to the surface. There were quarrels about money in the players' Cup pool and winger Jimmy Johnstone and captain Billy Bremner were fined for misconduct just a few days before the first match.

Scotland found themselves in the same Group Two as Zaire, the African rabbits of the competition. But instead of using them for target practice in the opening game they laboured to beat them 2–0 with goals from Peter

Lorimer and Joe Jordan. When Yugoslavia put nine past Zaire a few days later, the Scottish effort was put in its true perspective, and, although they drew 0–0 with Brazil and 1–1 with Yugoslavia, Scotland were eliminated.

Strangely, though, they were to be the only team not to suffer a defeat in these Finals. Even West Germany, the eventual winners, lost a group match 1–0 to East Germany, though some suspected they were attempting to manipulate the group placings so they would have an easier draw in the later stages.

The competition this time was organised on the usual four-group system. Then the leading two teams from each went through to two final pools which again competed on a league basis. The top team from each then played off for the Cup.

The West Germans were strongly fancied from the start. Apart from being the hosts, they had retained the nucleus of the European Championship team which had destroyed England 3–1 at Wembley two years earlier. But

The goal that won the World Cup for West Germany in 1974: Gerd Müller's shot speeds past Holland's Rudi Krol

the favourites were Holland, inspired by the dazzling Johan Cruyff, and playing their magical total football where every member of the team was an expert at both defence and attack and able to switch from one to the other at a moment's notice.

Holland cruised through their group interrupted only by a goalless draw with the impressive Swedes. That put them into a second pool of four which contained Brazil, East Germany and Argentina. Showing the full range of their extraordinary ability they crushed Argentina 4–0, East Germany 2–0 and Brazil 1–0 to enter the final without conceding a goal. Nobody was going to bet against them.

The West Germans, meanwhile, had entered a final pool containing Poland, Sweden and Yugoslavia. Only Poland provided stiff opposition – showing that England's failure against them was not such a disgrace after all. But they, too, fell 1–0 as the Germans collected maximum points to face the Dutch in the final at Munich.

Holland's team, built from their outstanding club sides Ajax and Feyenoord, made a spectacular start. In their very first attack Cruyff was upended by Hoeness and Wolverhampton butcher Jack Taylor bravely became the first referee to award a penalty in a World Cup final. Neeskens scored from the spot.

Twenty-five minutes later Jansen upended Hölzenbein, and Breitner equalised from the second penalty. The decision unnerved the Dutch. They lost their composure and, just before half-time, their chance of the Cup, as the deadly Müller crashed home the winner. Once again, the team to score first had lost the final.

The Road to Argentina

On March 7, 1976, a crowd of 4,250 turned up at Freetown to watch Sierra Leone beat Nigeria 5–1 in the opening match of the African extra preliminary round. The World Cup 1978 was under way.

There were immediate casualties. For reasons of pride, politics or plain pique, Central Africa, who had been paired with Zaire, withdrew. Sudan followed, then Tanzania, and finally, just three months after that opening game, Zaire, who had been drawn against Nigeria for the first round proper, also pulled out.

Still, the loss of four countries kept the African group nice and tidy, and Egypt and Tunisia, joint favourites to qualify, squared up to each other in front of a 90,000 crowd in Cairo, where Egypt won 3–1, and a crowd of 120,000 in Tunis, where Tunisia gained revenge by a 4–1 scoreline.

On December 11, 1977, 21 months after hostilities opened at Freetown, the African group of 38 nations had been whittled down to one winner – Tunisia. Egypt were pipped by one point into second place, and they in turn finished a point ahead of Nigeria. Tunisia collected five points from their four games, drawing at home with and then beating Nigeria away; and losing to and then finally beating Egypt in front of that mammoth 120,000 crowd.

The CONCACAF group comprises America North and Central and the Caribbean. In the Northern area the United States, Canada and Mexico all finished with four points. A heavily perspiring Mexico were gratefully top on superior goal difference and Canada won the play-off for second place, beating the United States 3–0. The Central area was won by Guatemala with eight points from El Salvador (seven), Costa Rica (six) and Panama (three).

From the three preliminary rounds for the Caribbean, Haiti and Surinam emerged as the top two and they joined Mexico and Canada and Guatemala and El Salvador for what, in the end, turned out to be a runaway win for Mexico. After their early frights the Mexicans found their true form and won all five of their games, scoring 20 goals while conceding only five. Haiti finished second with seven points; Canada and El Salvador tied for third place with five points; Guatemala collected three; and Surinam none.

South America, another three-group zone, produced, predictably enough, Brazil as winners of Group One against Paraguay and Colombia. Bolivia were Group Two winners against Uruguay and Venezuela, and Peru came out top against Chile and Ecuador to win Group Three. In the final eliminating round Brazil duly confirmed

A recent line-up from Brazil, winners of South America's qualifying Group One. Back row *(from left)*: Ze Maria, Leao, Amaral, Edinho, Toninho Cerezo, Rodrigues Neto, unidentified trainer. Front row: unidentified trainer, Gil, Isidoro, Roberto, Rivelino, Marcelo

world expectations by winning both their games to head the group comfortably with Peru also qualifying as runners-up. It is interesting that poor Bolivia, who began with such high hopes after fighting through the qualifying stages, were slaughtered 8–0 by Brazil and 5–0 by Peru. The Scots, who have Peru in their qualifying group in the Finals in Argentina, would do well to note that Brazil managed only a 1–0 win against them.

Hong Kong won the first Asian group, reduced to five nations by the withdrawal of Sri Lanka on November 13, 1975. They finished with a point' to spare over Singapore. Next, trailing each other by a single point, came Malaysia, Indonesia and Thailand.

The second Asian group was won by South Korea over Israel and Japan; the third group by Iran over Saudi Arabia and Syria; and the fourth group by Kuwait over Qatar and Bahrain. Here the United Arab Emirates, soon to become the desert domain for England's Don Revie, withdrew from the competition on January 15, 1977.

The Asian group winners were to play off against the Oceania section, which had been won by Australia. The Aussies qualified two points clear of New Zealand, with the Republic of China at the bottom of the group with nothing to show for their efforts. New Zealand twice beat the Chinese 6–0 while the Aussies won their encounters against them 3–0 and 2–1. Crowds for the Australia–New Zealand clashes were almost identical. There were 12,500 in Sydney, where the Aussies won 3–1, and only 500 fewer in Auckland, where the teams drew 1–1.

Five nations challenged for the qualifying place, eventually won by Iran with 14 points from eight games. Korea (10 points) were second; Kuwait (nine) third; Australia (seven) fourth; and Hong Kong (none) bottom. It was a great disappointment for the Aussies, who threw away a superb chance by losing 1–0 to Iran in Melbourne and 2–1 to Kuwait in Sydney. The Melbourne defeat was the bitterest pill because after Hassan Rowshan had scored for Iran, the team once managed by Frank O'Farrell, the former Manchester United manager, Dave Harding missed a penalty for Australia. Gloomy Aussie manager Jim Shoulder said after the game: "If that penalty had gone in we would have won comfortably. Iran had one chance and stuck it in." The Aussies came back bravely in their final games in Kuwait and Teheran. But both matches, played inside a week, were lost 1–0.

Meanwhile in Europe, where competition for places in Argentina was again to be the toughest, Poland, as expected in the light of their splendid performances in Germany in 1974, saw off Portugal, Denmark and Cyprus (who finished in that order) without too much trouble.

The Poles took the initiative right from the off and on October 16, 1976, won their first game in Portugal 2–0. In less than a year after that game, they were through, with only one point surrendered in six matches.

Things started quite brightly for Don Revie's England

Bettega (on the ground) watches as his shot beats England's Ray Clemence to give Italy their second goal in the qualifying match in Rome

in Helsinki in June, 1976. A 4–1 win over Finland, although it did not completely satisfy all the critics, was not an unreasonable beginning and gave little warning of the disasters to follow.

They came quickly, starting with a laboured 2–1 win over Finland at Wembley, where – quite reasonably in the light of the win in Helsinki – a glut of goals had been expected. As events turned out, the lack of goals was crucial.

Italy, the main challengers for the group, opened their account with a 4–1 win in Luxembourg and quickly followed up with a telling body blow, beating England 2–0 in Rome. A 5–0 win for England over Luxembourg at Wembley raised a flicker of hope, but Italy had every Englishman biting his fingernails again when they went to Helsinki and beat Finland 3–0.

Revie decided he had had enough, and in the summer, with two World Cup qualifying matches remaining, he resigned in favour of a job worth nearly £60,000 a year with the United Arab Emirates. Ron Greenwood, whose long association with West Ham had earned him a reputation as one of the best tacticians in the game, in addition to being a man dedicated to attractive football, became caretaker manager.

His first test, a 2–0 win in Luxembourg, had a mixed reception. While most admitted his task in the short time he had left was virtually impossible, there had been little to admire in the England performance. It had been, yet again, drearily pedestrian.

Italy, knowing that they had their challenger on the ropes, ended all the speculation with a 6–1 trouncing of Finland in Turin. What was to have been the crunch match – England *v*. Italy at Wembley – now really did not matter, except to the supreme optimists. England faced a mammoth task, requiring certainly no less than a six-goal winning margin. They responded magnificently with a hope-raising 2–0 victory which should have produced at least four goals. But still even that would not have been enough because Italy coasted to a 3–0 win over Luxembourg in their final match to win the group on a goal difference of 18–4 to England's 15–4.

Somewhere along the line England would have needed another four goals to have pipped the Italians, but there were few outside the squads assembled first by Revie and then by Greenwood who could say honestly that England deserved any better than they achieved. Perhaps the real difference between the teams was best pinpointed by Italy's captain and central defender, Giacinto Facchetti, on the eve of the match in Rome. He forecast: "We will beat England because we have patience and they have not. We will not panic if the goals do not come immediately. But England will. That difference in temperament means we will win."

As expected, Austria won Europe's Group Three, a point clear of East Germany with Turkey and Malta trailing at the bottom. Both games between the main challengers ended in 1–1 draws with 72,000 spectators in Vienna and 95,000 in Leipzig. British referee Tom Reynolds needed a police escort from the Vienna match after disallowing Austria what would have been the winning goal four minutes from the end. Rioting fans tried to burn down the stadium and Reynolds and his fellow Welshmen Gerald Morgan and John Davies, who were his linesmen, were locked in the referee's room "for safety" until more than an hour after the game ended.

Northern Ireland's bid in Group Four earned them only third place behind Holland, with 11 points, and Belgium, with six points. Danny Blanchflower's boyos collected their five points with a 2–2 draw in Rotterdam against Holland, a 2–0 win over Iceland and a 3–0 win over Belgium. But they threw away any outside chance they might have had in a 2–0 defeat by Belgium in Liège, a shocking 1–0 defeat by Iceland in Reykjavik and a 1–0 defeat by Holland in Belfast.

France, by no means a top power in European soccer, pipped Bulgaria by one point and Eire by three to qualify from Group Five, while Sweden saw off both Norway and Switzerland to head Group Six. Eire's hopes were smashed in an ugly, brawling match in Sofia, where four players – two from each side – were sent off during Bulgaria's 2–1 win. Arsenal's Liam Brady had stamped himself as a potential world-class player with the goal that beat France in the match immediately before, and so a win in Sofia would most certainly have secured qualification for Eire.

That the game is about temperament was underlined by the Scots on their way to qualifying from Group Seven. The danger team was Czechoslovakia and the signs were ominous when Scotland lost their opening encounter in Prague 2–0.

Mike Smith, the Englishman who manages Wales, always believed the Welshmen had a good chance of qualifying and he maintained that optimism even after losing 1–0 in Glasgow. It seemed he had a point when Wales drubbed the Czechs 3–0 at Wrexham, but the Scots came roaring back into the picture with a 3–1 revenge win over Czechoslovakia at Hampden Park and then, in what was to prove the crunch match, beat Wales 2–0 at Liverpool's Anfield ground.

Wales were handicapped in having to surrender home advantage because they had no ground meeting the required safety regulations large enough to stage the match. For 79 minutes there had been little between the teams but then a hand knocked away the ball in the penalty area and Monsieur R. Wurtz, the French referee, adjudged that the hand belonged to Wales's David Jones. The Welsh protested fiercely that the ball had been handled by a Scot and subsequent television pictures suggested they might well have been right. But M. Wurtz was adamant and Masson slotted the spot-kick home. While there are Welshmen who will go to their

Don Masson, whose penalty kick dashed the Welsh hopes at Anfield

graves believing a terrible injustice was done to them at Anfield on the night of October 12, 1977, they could have nothing but admiration for the goal that followed, a superb glancing header by Kenny Dalglish after a rather spectacular run on the right side of the field by Martin Buchan.

Spain won Group Eight from Rumania and Yugoslavia. Hungary beat Russia and Greece for the right to play Bolivia for the final qualifying place and cruised home with wins of 6–0 and 3–2. Spain had a violent 1–0 win over Yugoslavia in their final match in Belgrade. Four Spaniards and two Yugoslavs were booked by

English referee Ken Burns when fighting broke out among the players. Spanish striker Juanito was taken to hospital after being knocked out by a bottle thrown by a spectator.

So it ended. From early 1976 until the end of 1977 the world had played 251 football matches, all highly charged with emotion and some bitterness. Enemies had been made and very few friendships sealed in this series to find 14 nations to join Argentina, as the hosts, and West Germany, as the holders, for the Finals which open with the holders playing Poland in Buenos Aires on June 1.

The world's footballing nations, after licking their own personal wounds, could stand back and reflect on the fact that Tunisia, for example, had managed what England had failed to do – qualify.

But Scotland's tartan army of supporters had only one real problem – how to get to the World Cup Finals without a ticket! Because, somehow or other, they will be in Cordoba and Mendoza (where Scotland play their Group Four matches) in their thousands, singing "Flower of Scotland" and roaring "We are the people!" If raging patriotism and never-ending optimism won matches then the rest of the world might as well stay home and save their money!

The draw has given Scotland what looks to be an easy group, plus the advantage of having to play the strongest opposition, Holland, last on June 11, by which time the required target will be plain for all to see.

Peru – against whom Scotland open on June 3 – and Iran are the alleged weaklings in the group, but then so were Zaire in 1974 and it is sickening history to recall how Scotland failed to turn the screw on them. Peru, in fact, have an impressive record under their manager Marcus Calderon, who was assistant to Didi when Peru came so near to beating West Germany in the 1970 Mexico Finals. They had an 8–2 goal aggregate in their

Peru in action during their last World Cup tournament in 1970: goalkeeper Rubinos saves from West Germany's Gerd Müller

first South American qualifying group against Chile and Ecuador, then a 5–1 aggregate in the play-offs with Brazil and Bolivia, losing only 1–0 to Brazil.

Iran, in a five-nation Asian play-off with Australia, Kuwait, North Korea and Hong Kong, had a 10–2 aggregate. Iran are managed by Heshmet Mohadjerani, who was assistant to Frank O'Farrell when he had charge of the national team.

Ally MacLeod's greatest problem will be the physical one of covering the distance in an attempt to watch both teams and at the same time knit together his own squad for the British championships only ten days before the World Cup.

Remembering that the Scots are not always at their best against allegedly weak opposition and that the minnows have a reputation for causing upsets in the World Cup, neither Peru – largely a team of veterans – nor Iran should be underestimated. No doubt Mr MacLeod has heard first-hand from Mr O'Farrell that Iran are a "useful side", very fit and with three or four extremely good ball players in their ranks.

The Scots' clear-cut 3–1 destruction of Czechoslovakia, the European Champions, last September, produced some of the most exciting, co-ordinated football played in Britain for a long, long time. In a 20-minute spell before half-time Scotland played with a penetration and variety that surpassed anything Billy Bremner's team produced in West Germany in 1974. Springboard for that impressive performance was the midfield trio of Bruce Rioch, Don Masson and Asa Hartford. Now it remains to be seen if players like John Robertson, who has contributed so much to the success of Nottingham Forest, will reproduce their true form in the cauldron of World Cup soccer. Robertson has all the gifts of a classic Scottish winger – balance, change of pace, control and vision – plus a tactical sense which gives him the ability to drop back into midfield and still remain highly creative.

Some stark pointers have emerged in the build-up to the Finals. One is that Kuwait, for example, cannot be dismissed as a joke team. The progress they have made under that astute Brazilian Mario Zagalo was proved – even though it was a friendly – in their goalless draw with Wales and indicates there has been a rapid levelling-up in ability from the emerging Third World. Ron Greenwood believes it to be the case and so does Italy's Enzo Bearzot, who says: "There is no longer much difference in the athleticism of national teams. To win today you have to employ superior technique." It is a fact England, particularly, have failed to observe. Yet there remains the mystery of how Liverpool can be so consistently successful against Continental teams and England, even when laden with Liverpool players, so ineffective.

Another meaningful pointer on the road to Argentina has been the impressive consistency of holders West Germany. Helmut Schoen, now 63 and committed to retirement as team manager after Argentina, already has a record that sets him alongside the greatest managers in the history of the game. He took a team to the final in 1966, another to the semi-final in 1970 and sent out the winners in 1974. Now, without a real successor to Netzer and Overath in midfield and the irreplaceable Beckenbauer playing with New York Cosmos, he may gamble on Hans Müller, the little Stuttgart player, who can be devastating on his day.

Certainly the 20 players he took on the Latin American tour made a startling impact, convincingly defeating Argentina and Uruguay, clearly superior in their drawn match with Brazil and still strong enough, despite the stamina-sapping rarified atmosphere, to conclude their tour with a 2–2 draw against Mexico. They will again be hard to beat, for Schoen has added to their traditional game of muscle and lungs skills and techniques that are second to none.

Says Schoen: "We have raised our skills to the point where we feel inferior to nobody, not even the Brazilians. But, what is equally important, we have not discarded the best of our old ways, the strongest of our natural assets. We are fast and athletic footballers by nature, and speed will always be a key weapon for us. We break out of defence fast, and when things go wrong and our moves break down our players flood back behind the ball so quickly that danger is often smothered before it becomes serious. But the indispensable element in all our efforts to blend speed and athleticism with fine technique is vision. If I had to identify the hallmark of the football we try to play and the quality we hope may set us apart it would be the capacity to read the game at speed."

Though Schoen has followed a steady pattern for refining while confirming the identity of German football, he has not swerved from a basic formula of man-for-man marking with a sweeper, usually three midfield men, two attackers specialising in breaks wide on the flanks, and a strong central striker.

One assumes that Brazil, who have won their World Cups in places as far apart as Sweden, Chile and Mexico, will again justify their position as favourites by producing the strikers they so badly need. They have rarely failed in the past to unearth some rare talents and spring them on the world when it matters most.

Italy, certainly, appear to have found a gem in Paolo Rossi, a 21-year-old Tuscan who has been a huge success in recent internationals and threatens to depose Francesco Graziani. Rossi is a centre-forward with the ability to go it alone and conjure goals out of nothing. He has developed a deadly opportunism, essential in the Italian game, where the centre-forward has to fend for himself against close-marking defences.

Argentina themselves reckon to have the man who may well emerge as player of the series, fragile-looking José Daniel Valencia. Valencia plays for Talleres and was capped last year in the match against Russia. He is rated by both present manager Menotti and former international Humberto Maschio as the best player they have ever seen, which is some tribute when one has regard for the almost unending list of talent Argentina has supplied to Spain, Italy, France, Portugal, Brazil, Peru, Colombia and Mexico. There are 67 Argentinians playing in the Spanish League alone!

For Spain the Atletico Bilbao right-winger, 26-year-old Dani, has outshone the more favoured pair, Juanito and Lopez Afarte. Though on the small side he is a deadly accurate header of the ball and has shown plenty of fighting spirit at international level.

If Holland do not have Cruyff at centre-forward they may well turn to blond, 21-year-old Kees Kist of AZ 67, a strong, forceful player, dangerous in the air, whose temperament seems ideal. With an abundance of midfield talent to call upon, Holland could provide him with the sort of service that has seen him score five goals in a match.

A scene from Poland's match against Italy in the 1974 Finals:
Szarmach (white shirt) gets to grips with the Italian defence

Poland will have those 1974 dazzlers, Szarmach and Zmuda, with them again, and among the newcomers is bound to be 20-year-old inside forward Zbigniew Boniek, playing in midfield with the celebrated Deyna and Kasperczak. The lanky, red-haired Boniek gave the Manchester City defence a hard time when his team, Widzew Lodz, drew with them in the UEFA Cup at Maine Road last September.

Time for speculation is running short. There will, of course, be last-minute surprises before the 16 nations take up their action stations for what, for those who play, is the most testing and thrilling experience of their lives. Those of us who watch will be served up with a feast so rich in its content that the prospects of humdrum League soccer to follow will become almost unpalatable.

The fervent hope is that in Argentina the Scots, so steeped in the traditions of the game, will this time show the discipline that will enable them to give full vent to their vast flow of talents. They are, potentially, a great team. Had they been playing the Finals in Europe they would have had little to fear. But if they can successfully adjust to their surroundings and, perhaps more importantly, master their own sometimes abrasive character, they will return with pride.

In fact, if they simply do themselves justice that may well be enough to win.

Great Britain for the Cup?

It may not be the opportune moment to put the case for a Great Britain team to represent England, Northern Ireland, Scotland and Wales, but it may become a fact – however unpalatable to the Scots – at the FIFA conference which will be held soon after the end of hostilities in Argentina.

The member nations of soccer's governing body give scant regard to the fierce nationalism of the four home countries. To them we are one. One island. One country. And they feel we are getting four chances to their one of winning the World Cup – five, in fact, if one includes Eire, as most other nations tend to do.

That we have been able this far to retain our national individualism is due to two factors. The first is that Britain has always made four separate contributions to FIFA and the 150 member nations have grudgingly recognised that the "full house" internationals at stadiums like Wembley and Hampden Park have produced financial contributions of considerable importance to the survival of the international association. Indeed, it was the proceeds from the gate at the England versus the Rest of the World match at Wembley that provided FIFA with the money to continue after the Second World War.

The second factor in the survival of England, Northern Ireland, Scotland and Wales as separate entities was Sir Stanley Rous, who, after 28 years as secretary of the Football Association, served 12 years and eight months as president of FIFA. Sir Stanley was replaced by João

Havelange after the 1974 World Cup but remains a life president of football's world governing body.

It would be the greatest over-simplification of all time to say that Sir Stanley was a law unto himself. But he was. He is a man of impressive physical stature and such enormous vision that he was never out-manoeuvred by the pressure groups who demanded that our forces should be merged and just one team – Great Britain – be permitted to represent the United Kingdom.

But it is doubtful if even Sir Stanley could much longer fight off the increasing pressures to end our independence. For the growth of commercialism around the game has built up to such proportions that ticket sales scarcely matter any longer. The World Cup is now sport's biggest seller, the most demanded event of them all. FIFA can hardly fail now to stay solvent.

But with Scotland on the crest of a wave – even though the rest of the world claims, with some justification, that their best players are trained and groomed in the English First Division – the rest of Britain has precious little to offer.

Scots would perhaps agree that goalkeepers Peter Shilton and Ray Clemence with possibly Trevor Brooking and Dave Watson from England *might* strengthen their squad. They might also find the Arsenal duo Pat Jennings (Northern Ireland) and Liam Brady (Eire) acceptable. But there are few other players in the British Isles that Scotland would want to take with them to Argentina.

So, if there is ever to be an England in the World Cup again, what can be done to improve their dismal record since they won the trophy under Sir Alf Ramsey at Wembley in 1966?

First priority must be given to the creation of a premier, or super, league of 16 or 18 clubs. That would give room at the top for the men who would automatically be drawn into the premier league to take part in matches where they could develop their skills instead of all the

Pat Jennings of Arsenal and Northern Ireland: he would be a strong contender for a place in a Great Britain team

time playing in competitive games that have to be won, as in the present First Division.

We could still have as many leagues as might be necessary – five if you like – to carry on meeting the obligations the Football League has to the Pools companies. Continue, certainly, some form of promotion and relegation system that would allow any club talented enough to have access to the very top division.

A reduction in the number of competitive matches in the top division would reduce the strain on players and provide room for manoeuvre so that Ron Greenwood and his England managerial team could plan a campaign to involve greater use of international talents, from the youth team right through to the senior international squad.

The obvious flaw in the English game at the moment is the lack of individual skill. The First Division, of necessity perhaps, puts too great an emphasis on survival. Fear, promoted by amateur directors who control the destinies of great soccer clubs, has driven out individual flair. Defeat to so many becomes something of a personal affront and survival has attained an importance out of all proportion to the basic ingredients of the game.

The years characterised by this obsession for survival, even if it means just a lowly place in the First Division, have resulted in a predictability about the English game that has made the national team a lesser force in international circles than it has ever before been. It is sad to listen to foreign managers applauding only physical strength and determination in the English player where once they applauded his skill.

It may have all stemmed from 1966, when, buoyed up by winning the World Cup, England clung for too long to a group of players who had proved themselves right for that one occasion. England's victory may also have caused the introduction of what is perhaps the most ruinous tactic of all – pattern coaching, with everyone conforming to a method. Coaching can be effective only if it is given over to people who have regard for the needs of the individual player.

Another reason for sadness is the way in which England allows the talents of its consistently successful youth team to be dissipated. Year after year they go out and win the European tournament that is often tagged the "Little World Cup" and then come home to disband to their respective clubs, rarely to be heard of again.

Such an asset would be exploited by other countries, who would keep their team together, give them games against the Under 23's and thus develop them as a recruiting ground for the senior internationals. There is hope now that under Ron Greenwood this asset will not much longer be frittered away.

Overall, the English have got to become better ball players. They have got to learn to master the basic skills in the way the Scots and so many of the European and South American players have learned, so that they do not waste that precious split second bringing the ball under control and getting it on their "best" foot.

While the degree of efficiency achieved by England's goalkeepers and defenders is still greatly admired, the fact remains that defenders do not win matches. They may stop the other side winning but they cannot make the decisive thrust which is the difference between stopping someone winning and winning with sheer brilliance.

England managers and coaches have to become imaginative again in what, after all, is the most vital aspect of the game – goal scoring. They must go into games with a positive desire to win rather than the dreary philosophy of playing not to lose, which is a lot to ask when one has regard for the number of managers who have lost their jobs because their team has been relegated.

But English soccer will succeed again only when the power of the amateur director is diminished and the manager is able to feel that his livelihood will be in no way jeopardised if he encourages his players to develop skill with the ball, to control it, to dribble it and to pass it in the manner of a Tom Finney or a Stanley Matthews.

The problems facing England cause nothing but glee to the Scots. Sure, they had a similar decline in their playing standards, but they came out of it almost immediately after England won the World Cup. England's success may well have been the spur.

That this was so is open to dispute, but it was on May 25, 1967, in Lisbon that Jock Stein spoke up for all those fierce patriots who firmly believe Scotland can survive on its own. Stein, just 27 months after becoming manager of Celtic, won the European Cup and became the first of three managers from Britain to win soccer's second most prestigious trophy.

He did it with an all-Scots team groomed in a league that so often is little more than a two-horse race. Only deadly rivals – and another of the world's truly great soccer clubs – Glasgow Rangers are consistently the team to beat.

Stein's triumph in Lisbon was a tremendous shot in the arm for pure soccer. Italy – and, to a degree, Europe – had been dominated and bullied by Helenio Herrera's Inter-Milan, who had scornfully rampaged through the Continent, stifling the skills of brilliant individuals with such a deadly-dull defensive blanket that, had it prospered much longer, would surely have killed off the game as a spectacle.

Herrera was the new emperor – arrogant, efficient, merciless, commanding a team of highly disciplined robots. Stein, on the other hand, was the upstart, the junior, about to be given a lesson to remember.

But Herrera lost all along the line. Before the kick-off he even delayed sending out his team in the hope that the Scots would be nervously waiting in Lisbon's red-hot cauldron, sweltering in a temperature in the high eighties. But Stein refused to leave the cool dressing-room unless the teams walked out together. In the end the Italians gave in.

Then Stein set Jimmy Johnstone, the wee, red-headed right-winger, on them. For 30 minutes the little Scot ran the Italian defence ragged, tormenting, tantalising and finally terrorising them into submission with a display of brilliance and stamina that could have come straight out of a book entitled *All the Best from Scotland*.

Perhaps no such book has been written, but Johnstone certainly supplied a splendid opening chapter that day. Despite going behind to a dubious penalty Celtic won 2–1 and in so doing moved Bill Shankly, that equally famous Scot who masterminded so many successes for Liverpool, to pronounce: "Celtic have shown the world today that soccer, *real* soccer, is about skill, enterprise, inventiveness

Jimmy Johnstone of Celtic and Scotland: his performance was decisive in Britain's first European Cup triumph

and entertainment. The world should give thanks to Jock Stein for killing off for all time a type of game that had become a disease.''

Next it was Manchester United, with a slightly less formidable task because they played their final at Wembley, who became European Champions. Again the man at the helm was a Scot, Sir Matt Busby, and although Stein was to move mountains in his first ten years at Celtic, winning the Championship nine times, the Cup six times and every other tournament Glasgow could offer, Matt did perhaps even more.

He had built a magnificent Championship side soon after the war and, while many thought it had still to reach its peak, he dismantled it. In its place came a group of youngsters of such electrifying talents that almost overnight they became household names as the "Busby Babes". That brilliant team was destroyed in a plane crash at Munich in 1958, but Busby, himself terribly injured, returned to Old Trafford to rebuild again and eventually to capture the trophy he most coveted – the European Cup – just ten years after the Munich tragedy.

Last year it was the turn of Liverpool, who, although now managed by Bob Paisley, owed much of their character and style to the devoted attentions (some would add supplications) of Bill Shankly.

It might be argued that the Liverpool team were the least skilled of the three British victors. Certainly they had not the spectacular individuals of Manchester United (who can follow Bobby Charlton, George Best and Denis Law?) but that is not the point at issue here. What is inarguable is the fact that only three times has the European Cup come to Britain and each time to a club managed, or formulated, by a Scot.

So, if the home countries are forced to unite to play under the Great Britain banner in the future, will the rest of the world adjudicate on how big a say Scotland must have?

They will justifiably not settle for a minor role, because they are currently producing the most exciting players and, historically, have given British soccer its most successful managers.

Scotland are hardly likely to be crying for England, Ireland or Wales out there in Argentina!

America's Soccer Challenge

New Yorkers kicked down cinema doors to watch the 1966 World Cup and the big-dollar boys were suddenly awakened to the fact that the United States had nothing in their sports arenas to match the worldwide appeal of soccer.

Audiences in excess of 500 million were watching the action live, thanks to satellites and the ever-improving technology of TV.

A film called *Goal*, shot in England and recording every vital kick of Sir Alf Ramsey's triumph, shattered all the established prejudices that regarded any sports film as bad box office. *Goal* climbed into the top ten ratings wherever it was shown.

America was made suddenly aware that, Olympic Games aside, they were not on sport's international totem pole. Their code of football, their basketball and their baseball were never going to sell to the world the way soccer does.

The Americans were determined to get in, but they had some early shocks when they quickly found that money, even in seemingly limitless quantities, was no substitute for tradition. Unlike instant coffee you could not just pour on boiling water – or, in this case, dollars – and come up with a palatable result.

The Americans started by importing European players. Those from Britain were mainly from the lower leagues and often nearing the end of their careers. But it was still believed in the States that by catering for their many ethnic groups – Italians, Germans, Hungarians, Poles and the rest – America could arouse an overnight interest in a game that, while it excited the world, had left the United States cold.

The initial experiment petered out, a costly failure. The message was spelled out yet again: in America, as everywhere else, soccer needs genuine patriotism. To most Americans the planners were proving what they always felt, that it was a game for foreigners played only by immigrants.

They barely noticed the revolution going on in their own schools. Soccer was spreading like a forest fire. Here, said the American youngster, was a game anyone could play. You didn't have to be a seven-foot giant, as basketball requires, or a near-gorilla, like those who are the backbone of gridiron. This was a sport that gave the little fellow the same opportunities to attain fame and fortune as the giants of the other American sports.

The man who laid the foundations for the day, perhaps only ten years away, when America becomes the new centre of world soccer is Phil Woosnam, the Welsh international inside-forward who played for Orient, West Ham and Aston Villa. He went to the States on the wave of euphoria England's World Cup win had aroused, but after a couple of years he was ready to quit and go home.

The Americans were doing it all wrong, trying to win from the middle instead of building from the bottom. Luckily, Woosnam was appointed Commissioner for the North American Soccer League and overnight had the strongest voice in US football.

He won the chance to start again, his way. He turned to the schools but discovered that the American education system does not take the same full responsibility for school sports education as the British system does. There it is more of a community project, and so Woosnam had to get out in the sticks, direct his energies at the small communities outside the big cities and sell the game to parents.

They responded immediately. They liked the fact that kitting out Junior for soccer was considerably less expensive than kitting him out for baseball or gridiron. Most of all they liked the fact that it did not matter if Junior was a bit on the weedy side. He could still get into the game.

Interest snowballed and the tribute to Woosnam's efforts lies in the fact that in many American schools soccer is now the major sport. In Dallas, Texas, alone there are more than 50,000 youngsters playing the game and the American Youth Soccer Organisation, founded in 1964 with just nine teams, now has more than 7,000

They have started summer camps. The George Logan California camp provides five one-week sessions at the University of San Diego where boys – and girls – from eight to 18 live and eat in student housing and are coached on the university's four athletics fields.

The Americans now have a sound base and one which is getting stronger each year. The game is outstandingly popular in the schools and students are emerging with enough talent for the game to suggest that an all-American team might be a serious challenger for the 1982 World Cup Finals.

Woosnam took with him to the States the advantage of Britain's 100 years of experience in the game and he was determined it would never become in America the man-only sport it has been for so long over here. Soccer had to be made acceptable to the entire family unit, and, although admission charges are four times higher than they are in Britain, the American family has the advantage of superb stadiums and a tremendous climate through the entire season from April until August.

Nor are the Americans afraid to experiment. They could never, for example, understand the reasoning behind allowing games to end as draws. So they got rid of them. If there is a tie at the end of 90 minutes they play a deciding seven and a half minutes each way. The first team to score in that extra time wins, but if the game is still tied at the end of 15 minutes they have a penalty decider or, as they prefer to call it, a "shoot-out".

Thus every game has a result. But they are looking for more excitement, and so they want now to introduce a midfield zone, 20 yards each side of the halfway line, where the offside rule cannot operate. They may even experiment with goals widened two feet to 26 feet with the crossbar raised six inches to eight and a half feet.

The North American Soccer League started with nine

Three international superstars who, playing for New York Cosmos, have done much to popularise soccer in the United States: Beckenbauer of West Germany is flanked by Pele of Brazil and Chinaglia of Italy

clubs, grew to 24 and eventually will have 32. But the real boom, the one that has got everybody talking World Cup, began when Pele joined New York Cosmos, the club backed by the powerful Warner organisation.

Suddenly, in the eyes of the entire nation, soccer was given credibility. For here was the greatest player in the world right in amongst them. The Cosmos ended their 1977 campaign playing regularly in front of crowds totalling more than 70,000. Ten years earlier they were averaging just over 5,000.

Players like George Best, Rodney Marsh, Bobby Moore, Mike England, Tommy Smith, Charlie Cooke, Gordon Banks, Phil Beal and a host more from Britain were Woosnam's front-liners in his big sell. But it was Pele who finally gave the game the status Woosnam had worked so hard to obtain. Now the better coaches and managers are being tempted to build on the foundations so carefully laid by Woosnam and cemented by Pele. Top players, too, are looking with more and more longing towards the West, where America is building such a soccer skyscraper that it seems there will be no limit to the pinnacles it will achieve.

Arsenal chairman Denis Hill-Wood warned long ago that if soccer ever really took off in America there would be few nations who could hope to live with them. It is not without significance that the British, who started going there as teachers, are now making the journey as students. They want to see for themselves how the Americans sell the game to the public, to commerce and to the media.

In that field they are already light years ahead of Britain. The fact they will soon be turning out their own Georgie Bests from their high schools makes it very difficult to believe they will not soon become a major power in the game.

The Final Sixteen

Argentina

Colours: Light blue and white vertical striped shirts, black shorts, white stockings.

No one will be under more pressure than 39-year-old Cesar Luis Menotti, boss of the Argentinian national team, when those fervent fans flock into Buenos Aires. He will be expected to produce miracles and he has already been often reminded that the host nation is expected to do well.

Both Sweden (in 1958) and Chile (1962) rose to the occasion when they hosted the Finals and played way above their expected potential for Sweden to reach the final and Chile the semi-finals.

Nothing less will satisfy Argentina. In fact they have set their sights on emulating England and West Germany, who were both winners when they played in front of their own fans in 1966 and 1974 respectively.

It will be remembered, too, that England did not make an impressive start and really began to click only in the semi-final against Portugal, while West Germany actually lost a match to, of all people, their less prosperous neighbours East Germany.

Menotti has, unquestionably, many talented players to call on, but it remains to be seen whether the notoriously fragile temperament of the Argentinians will for once match the big occasion.

Another problem has been the misuse of natural footballing ability. In the past the Argentinians have

Argentina's skilful right-winger René Houseman, a key member of manager Menotti's squad

tended to delight in pretty, but too often ineffective, ball-juggling and intricate passing movements that are frequently punished when they break down.

Menotti had to make changes to meet the modern demands of the game and he has slowly introduced a more direct style while attempting to retain some of the charm and originality so revered by Argentinian fans.

Results against visiting European sides last summer, while not wholly satisfactory, did suggest that some progress has been made.

The defeat by West Germany was not a total disaster, because it showed Menotti that the best European teams are strong enough to succeed in South America and that he would have to make use of the players who were carving out very good livings in France and Spain.

The "absentees" are a sore point. Rather like those Scots who resent the selection of "Anglos" (those players under contract to English League clubs) there is a body of opinion in Argentina that would have all absentees ostracised.

But opinion is swinging towards their recall and with France and Spain both qualified many of them will be available for the "friendlies" from which Menotti will make his final selection.

He has already pencilled in the names of 14 players from Argentinian clubs, including Gatti, Carrascosa, Killer, Houseman and Bertoni. In addition he has asked for the release of Ayala from Atletico Madrid, Mario Kempes, the 23-year-old top scorer of the Spanish League, from Valencia, and full-back Wolff from Real Madrid. Also he wants from France the St Etienne trio, Piazza, Bargas and Bianchi.

"With these players", says Menotti, "we would have an excellent chance of winning the World Cup." If his team does win, he will have fulfilled the dreams of Gauchos everywhere.

Austria

Colours: White shirts, black shorts, black stockings.

Austria's team will be on £500 a point in the Finals, but it is unlikely that such inducements will make them rich. They provided one of the major surprises in the qualifying competition by knocking out East Germany, but both

Spain and Brazil would seem too strong for them in their group in Argentina.

Austria's main problem is one of morale. So many of their better players are with rich, fashionable clubs in other countries that petty jealousies mar most international get-togethers. New manager Helmut Senekowitz was tempted to leave out these foreign legionnaires from his World Cup squad but he knows he needs them if Austria are to make any impression in the Finals.

Of the players who have stayed loyal to Austrian clubs, Hans Krankl is the outstanding international. The 24-year-old centre-forward is built like a tank and his robust, no-nonsense approach – similar to that of Tottenham's Bobby Smith – has brought him 31 caps and the Austrian Footballer of the Year award in each

Austria's powerful centre-forward Hans Krankl

of the past four years. His powerful style was altogether too much for little Malta in the World Cup qualifying round and he scored six goals in the 9–0 rout. Krankl's main feedman is 22-year-old Herbert Prohaska, a skilful midfield player who appeared in all six World Cup qualifying games.

The other home-grown star is right-back Robert Sara, a tough-tackling defender who could, generously, be called uncompromising. Welsh winger Leighton James might have a different adjective after the harsh tackling Sara subjected him to during an international between the two countries at Wrexham last year.

The remainder of the Austrian cream will carry an "imported" label. In midfield the two "Bergers", Hattenberger from Stuttgart and Hickersberger from Dusseldorf, are the engine-room of the team. Both are highly experienced, quality performers and it was their understanding which so effectively stifled the East Germans in their two 1–1 qualifying draws.

Up front Krieger from Bruges, Jara from Duisberg and Kreuz from Feyenoord provide the firepower alongside Krankl. Kreuz, who now plays with former West Ham favourite Clyde Best in Holland, is particularly deadly in the air.

But the team is a far cry from that fabulous *Wunderbar* side of the 1930s. It is the first time Austria have qualified since 1954, when they finished third, beating Uruguay 3–1 in the play-off. Getting there again this time is their glory – anything else will be a bonus.

Brazil

Colours: Yellow shirts with green trim, blue shorts, white stockings with blue and yellow tops.

No nation takes the World Cup more seriously than Brazil. No manager gets such absolute control. Since February 27, Claudio Coutinho, a 40-year-old ex-army officer, has had all Brazil's World Cup "possibles" under his care.

The three-month period of preparation will have been used for training sessions, a tour of Europe – including the April date against England at Wembley – and warm-up matches against lesser opponents in Brazil.

When Coutinho came over to Europe on a spying tour he reported back to his faithful millions: "We have nothing to fear in Europe. It will be an all-South American final in Argentina." Even with Brazil's pedigree, that forecast ranks on a par with Sir Alf Ramsey's declaration back in 1963 that England would win the World Cup in 1966. Coutinho had better be just as right as Ramsey was!

Brazil, having thrilled us all with their phenomenal skills and inventiveness while winning the 1970 World Cup, hugely disappointed four years later in Germany when, doubtless remembering the rough treatment they received in England – particularly from Portugal – they changed to a mundane, safety-first system.

This completely out-of-character performance gained them fourth place in Germany and very few bouquets. They are certain to revert to their natural, almost careless, grace and the flowing football it brings when they play before the Argentinians, and the prospect of a Brazil in full flow again is something worth waiting for.

Coutinho signified his intentions when, following the exodus of such stars as Luis Pereira and Leivinha, he slapped a ban on further exports and then named a mammoth squad of 72 players whom he deemed as "untouchables".

The squad will of course be narrowed down as the shape of the eventual team starts to emerge, but it is virtually certain that an imaginative midfield will be cunningly marshalled by Roberto Rivelino, the former winger, who has lost none of his dynamic shooting power. Rivelino is now the provider rather than the executioner.

Roberto Rivelino of Brazil: now switched from a forward role into midfield

That role has gone to Zico, scorer of 63 goals in one season of domestic football. Sharing the midfield with Rivelino will be another budding Brazilian superstar, Antonio Carlos Corezo from Belo Horizonte.

Leao is likely to be in goal and the 22-year-old Filho in a defence that is sure to contain the muscular Luis Pereira, reckoned by many to be the best centre-back in the world. Francisco Marinho is another certain defender, while Roberto has only to repeat the high-scoring performances he has already given in friendly matches to earn the right to lead the attack.

Brazil have had, inevitably, to toughen up their defence, for, despite Coutinho's promise, there are plenty of players in the European pack alone that could give them a lot of trouble. But if we are to see again the sort of Brazil that carried all before them in Mexico, then Argentina will have more than done its duty to world football.

France

Colours: Blue shirts, white shorts, red stockings.

It seems a little odd that France, who originated the idea of some sort of global soccer tournament when that great Frenchman Jules Rimet was president of FIFA, have never ever attained the status of a major world footballing power.

The best they ever did was in Sweden in 1958 when Raymond Kopa inspired the French team to reach the semi-finals. Since then only the superb performances of St Etienne in European Cup competitions have given French fans, starved of any really outstanding success, some sort of hope.

Now it has all changed and there is unswerving optimism that France will at least reach the last eight and possibly emerge as the real surprise of the tournament.

Inevitably, comparisons are being made between the present young squad and that magical side of 20 years ago when the inside-forward trio of Kopa, Fontaine and Piantoni were the most dominant and talented formation in Europe.

Manager Michel Hidalgo will have no part of that debate. Tactics, attitudes and playing methods have changed drastically and it is doubtful if in today's team there would even be room for such a specialist as was outside-left Vincent.

Vincent is still spoken of with the same sort of awe Englishmen use when remembering the magic of Stanley Matthews, but for Hidalgo there is no going back. He says: "It is a magnificent feeling that I am in charge of a

The French team which lined up against Bulgaria for the 1977 qualifying match in Paris. Back row *(from left)*: Rey, Janvion, Bathenay, Bossis, Tresor. Front row: Rocheteau, Lacombe, Platini, Guillou, Six

team capable of reaching great heights of excellence. They are young but they have immense moral and physical courage."

When Hidalgo talks of his goalkeeper, André Rey – "a bastion, a tower of strength, a man who cannot be broken and one who gives the entire team a solid base" – he puts Rey in a category with Gordon Banks and Russia's Yashin, and if that is a true assessment then certainly the French base is sound.

They do have a brilliant sweeper in Tresor, the coloured player from Marseille, and are well served in defence by Gerard Janvion, Patrice Rio and Bossis.

Michel Platini, 23-year-old Player of the Year, is perhaps the finest footballer France has produced since the Kopa era. When he recently got married his club, Nancy, received special permission to postpone their League match so that his team-mates could be present!

Platini creates and scores goals with equal ease and if ever he went on the transfer list the bidding throughout Europe would begin at £750,000.

His main rival as a national pin-up is Dominique Rocheteau, a sort of Gallic George Best, who plays a guitar and mesmerises on the wing. He may not have the consistency Best had at his peak but he gets the same level of adulation and has to hide himself away in a country farmhouse, guarded by a huge alsatian dog, to escape all his female admirers.

France go to Argentina scarcely rated – which is a help – but full of confidence. They have the players and, at last, the know-how to become the surprise team of the tournament.

West Germany

Colours: White shirts with black trim, black shorts, white stockings.

No nation has had more success in world football during the post-war years than West Germany. After their victory in Switzerland in 1954 they were beaten finalists, semi-finalists and winners again in three consecutive World Cup bids between 1966 and 1974.

They also won the European Championship in 1972 and very nearly won it again four years later when, in a thrilling comeback against Czechoslovakia in Belgrade, Uli Hoeness blasted a penalty kick over the crossbar.

The transformation in German football over what is still a relatively short period is little less than breathtaking. Before the war they were nonentities and England used to pick them off, home and away, with almost regular monotony.

Their game then was strictly amateur but with Teutonic thoroughness and almost regimented planning they succeeded in putting the interests of the national side way above those of their clubs.

There was no mysterious inborn talent, no sudden awakening to modern tactics. Just a man named Helmut Schoen, a former pupil and assistant to Sepp Herberger who started the ball rolling with a shock victory over Hungary in 1954.

Schoen is a firm believer in continuity – "When you have got it right, keep it right", he says – and he has already named his successor, his own assistant, Jupp Derwall, who will take over the reins when Schoen retires after Argentina.

Schoen works closely with the German clubs and has persuaded them to play the same system and style as his national team. So when he picks a newcomer the player slots into the system as if born to it. Testimony comes in the form of Germany's record since Beckenbauer left to play for New York Cosmos. To most nations a player of Beckenbauer's tremendous talents would be irreplaceable, but to Germany his absence has been hardly noticeable.

When Gerd Müller, the man who ended England's hopes in extra time in the 1970 Mexico World Cup, retired from international football his namesake, Dieter Müller, stepped in and immediately scored a hat-trick.

The German method is all-action, total football with a

Two West German veterans of 1970 and 1974 who will be campaigning again in Argentina: captain Berti Vogts *(left)* and goalkeeper Sepp Maier

great deal of running off the ball and solid, physical contact. They build up slowly from the back with positive passing to players ever running into position. Giving away the ball through a bad pass is the cardinal sin and no one commits that very often.

Schoen has already reserved eight places for Argentina. Sepp Maier will be in goal, Berti Vogts and Dietz at full-back, Bonhof and Flohe in midfield, Ambrawczik on the right flank and Klaus Fischer as central striker. Manfred Kaitz, the sweeper from Hamburg, is proving an excellent replacement for Beckenbauer, but at centre-back Schoen will have to decide on Rüssmann or the return of the veteran Schwarzenbeck.

He has four candidates for the vacant midfield place and can choose from Bongartz, Beer, Burgsmüller or Hölzenbein, who can also play on the left wing. Challengers for that spot are Volkert, Seel and Rummenigge.

It seems that everywhere Schoen looks he sees a winner. His only problem is picking the right one at the right moment.

Holland

Colours: Orange shirts, white shorts, orange stockings.

Four years ago the Dutch threatened to dominate the world with their exciting new concept of "total" football. As recently as February last year they won the admiration of a 90,000 Wembley crowd by the smooth, stylish way they beat England 2–0. Yet Holland set out for Argentina with little neutral support for their chances of winning the World Cup for the first time.

The reason is that they will be without Johan Cruyff. The tall, lithe striker has maintained ever since he just failed to steer Holland to success in 1974 that he would not be appearing in any more World Cup Finals.

His motives have been the subject of fierce debate. Some maintained that he was worried by the prospect of intimidatory tackles in a country which has a frightening reputation for violence on and off the pitch. Others suggested that he was opening the way for a financial inducement in keeping with his status as undisputed successor to Pele as the world's top soccer attraction. But the most likely explanation is that Cruyff feared he might be the target for a kidnap attempt, despite the reported pledge by the Argentinian terrorists of an "armistice" for the duration of the series.

As Cruyff earns about £300,000 a year with the Spanish club Barcelona and could collect another fortune by accepting an offer from New York Cosmos, who have been wooing him for some time, money clearly has little bearing on the situation. Nor should he be daunted by any football opposition – his fantastic acceleration has always provided him with adequate protection. Whatever the reason for Cruyff's decision Holland's Austrian-born team manager Ernst Happel reluctantly omitted him from his squad of 40 probables. Of course, that still leaves Holland with a host of talent to call upon.

The superb Johan Neeskens, Cruyff's team-mate at Barcelona, can dominate the midfield against any opposition, the mighty Ajax left-back Rudi Krol can steady a defence in the most harrassing of situations, and Jan Peters, who scored both Holland's goals at Wembley last year, is developing into one of the most menacing strikers in the world.

Peters makes a significant point when he stresses that Holland's whirlwind style – massed attack one moment, reinforced defence the next – is perfectly suited to compensate for the loss of any individual. "Let's forget about Cruyff. We don't depend on him. We're an eleven-man team", says Peters.

The problem is: will Holland be able to field their best eleven? For, apart from Cruyff, several leading players have hinted that they are not too happy about the pros-

Holland's Robbie Rensenbrink: not too enthusiastic about the prospect of this year's tournament

pect of subjecting themselves to what will be a daunting, closely supervised month following an intensive preparation period. Robbie Rensenbrink, the splendid Anderlecht forward who was one of Holland's 1974 stars in West Germany, has admitted to friends that he is not overjoyed at the thought of playing in Argentina.

Holland have the talent to succeed – but do they have the will?

Hungary

Colours: Red shirts, white shorts, green stockings.

Hungary recalled the old fox, Lajos Baroti, now 63 years old, to try to lead them out of a 20-year wilderness of mediocrity back to the world status they enjoyed in the days of Puskas and Co. in the 1950s.

Baroti, in charge when Hungary qualified in 1958, 1962 and 1966, left the national side to go into club management and the immediate result was that the cherry-red jerseys of those once-magical Magyars were not seen in Mexico in 1970 and Germany in 1974.

But they are back now and Hungary, a small country so rich in footballing traditions, has never ceased rejoicing. And perhaps now the ghosts of that famous team which so nearly won the World Cup in Switzerland in 1954 will cease to haunt the Hungarians. Since those times players have never been allowed to forget the epic deeds of their famous predecessors and for years Hungarian footballers have been suffering from inferiority complexes.

The devotion of the Hungarian fan to his national team is quite remarkable. Ask him whether he would rather see his club side do the double or his national team win the World Cup and the answer comes back unhesitatingly . . . the World Cup.

Evidence of this fervent patriotism was overwhelmingly demonstrated after Hungary had beaten Russia to qualify for a play-off against Bolivia. More than 30,000 people marched through the streets of Budapest singing, dancing and crying with joy. And after Hungary had beaten Bolivia 6–0 at home and 3–2 at La Paz to qualify for Argentina a cartoon in one of the Hungarian newspapers showed Napoleon talking to manager Baroti. The caption had Baroti saying: "Did you ever experience 100,000 people chanting 'Thank you, Uncle Lajos?' "

That was immediate success for the old maestro.

Hungarian hopefuls for Argentina. Back row *(from left)*:
Meszaros, Kovacs, Kocsis, Toth, Gujdar. Second row:
Kereki, Pusztai, Pinter, Rab. Third row: Fazekas, Torocsik,
Zombori, Varadi. Front row: Martos, Balint, Halasz, Nagy

Suddenly the sinking ship was buoyant again.

Baroti says: "We hit rock-bottom when we lost to
Wales at home – and I mean no disrespect to Mike Smith
and his gallant team when I say that – and I took over.
I made wholesale changes in the team, opting for younger
players and insisting on a settled team. I ignored club
form and sometimes the national team appeared not to
field the best players. But we built a team – in the real
sense."

Baroti relies on a sound and solid defence in which Zoltan Kereki performs a sweeper-attacker role very much in the style of West Germany's Beckenbauer.

In midfield he has hard-working Sandor Pinter and up front the highly experienced Laszio Fazekas and goal-scorer Bela Varadi. But the boys who can tip the scales either way are Tibor Nyilasi and Andras Torocsik. Both are 23 years of age and both are inconsistent. On their day Nyilasi, in midfield, and Torocsik, up front making and scoring goals with nonchalant arrogance, can be absolutely devastating. Ally MacLeod is so impressed he has even tipped Hungary to win the World Cup.

But in the red-hot cauldron of Buenos Aires and Mar del Plata the Hungarians will find themselves in a different ball game to the pretty-pretty and outmoded central European football at which they have become masters again.

Iran

Colours: Green shirts, white shorts, red stockings.

Iran, playing in their first World Cup, are undoubtedly the strongest side to emerge from Asia since the 1966 North Koreans. The sincerity of their ambition to become a genuine world soccer power was endorsed with the appointment of Frank O'Farrell as national team manager. Much of the success for the foundation of a solid Iran challenge is due to O'Farrell, who handed over the reins to Heshmet Mohadjerani, his assistant for two years, when he decided to return to British football.

Ali Parvin, 31-year-old Iranian skipper, who directs operations from midfield, has been capped 82 times and in a fulsome tribute to O'Farrell credits the former Manchester United manager's enthusiasm and organising ability for much of the success the newly formed Iran Federation has achieved over the past three years.

Testimony to the skill of their players is shown in results they gained last year – a 1–1 draw with Argentina and a goalless draw with Rumania. Bayern Munich have tried unsuccessfully to lure left-winger Reza Adelkhani into their ranks and several Spanish clubs are keen to sign right-back Hassan Nazari.

Officially the Iranians are amateurs, but rumour has it

Iran's captain Ali Parvin: hoping to cause a few surprises

that they were paid a bonus of £10,000 per man for qualifying for the Finals. Against their chances of success in Argentina are their limited experience at international level plus the fact they play most of their football on hard pitches in extreme heat. The conditions they will play under in June will be completely foreign to them. But they have sufficient "goodies" in their pack to cause a few surprises.

"Old man" of the squad is Anokanik Eskandarian, who is 36 and usually plays at left-back. He was a regular in all the qualifying games and is vastly experienced, having also played in the 1976 Iran Olympic team.

Nasrollah Abdolahi, a central defender, has also been one of Iran's key players and at 24 has already made 18 appearances for his country. But the nation's hero is striker Ghaffur Jahani, a 27-year-old who was top scorer in the qualifying matches with five goals, including the one that clinched Iran's ticket for Argentina.

Ebrahim Ghassempour, a 21-year-old midfield player with 20 international appearances already to his credit, took part in Real Madrid's seventy-fifth anniversary tournament and has been a key performer in Iran's recent successes. So, too, has Hossein Kazerani, a 28-year-old central defender who has been a regular choice for the past 20 internationals.

Hassan Nabawy, 22-year-old goalkeeper drafted into the side last year, has had experience at intermediate international level and also took part in the Real Madrid anniversary matches along with Saham Murfakerai, a 27-year-old defender who was also in the Olympic side.

It is to be hoped that Hassan Roshan will be fully fit and included in the Iran line-up, because he is the sort of striker who might well win a lot of fans in Argentina. He is 22 and scored in the vital match against Australia in Melbourne. He also scored twice against South Korea but missed the final two qualifying matches through injury.

Italy

Colours: Blue shirts, white shorts, blue stockings with white rings at top.

We have already seen two faces of Italy – the one that beat England in Rome and the one that lost at Wembley. Now we await the third, and most telling, face.

Will it look something like that of Holland? Manager Enzo Bearzot hopes so. His dream is to free the Italians of all their inhibitions, to rid them of their boringly negative defensive style and to give them a more classic image which will also provide what has for so long been the missing ingredient – entertainment.

Holland play the sort of football he would like to see from Italy, but he confesses it would take a decade to perfect the flowing grace of the Dutchmen. So he has taken the 1974 Poland side as his blueprint – two strong centre-backs, a fluent midfield and strikers able to get back and help out in defence.

The tall Bearzot, a most likeable man, came to his conclusions for a "new Italy" in the first half of the match against England in New York in the summer of last year. "We were leading 2–0 and playing some very

Two of Italy's world-class players: striker Roberto Bettega *(left)* and goalkeeper Dino Zoff

attractive football. Then we had a most confusing second half and eventually lost 3–2. After the game I went into the dressing-room and told the players that in future the national team would play as we did in the first half or I would hand in my resignation."

It was a decisive moment for Bearzot and he could only hope the players would back him. They did and although they are perhaps only halfway towards attaining the goal Bearzot has set for them it is not easy to complete a revolution among clubs who doggedly stay faithful to a dreadful defensive system.

When the Italians do step out of their hideous strait-jacket they can be highly entertaining and easily capable of emulating their predecessors, who won the World Cup twice in pre-war years (1934 and 1938) and were runners-up in Mexico in 1970. But if they become frightened out of their rhythm – as they were by the North Koreans in England in 1966 – then their Latin temperament betrays them and they are led into awful errors which could have violent consequences in front of the volatile Argentinians.

One of Italy's outstanding assets is Bettega, possibly the best header of a ball in the world game today. He, with Graziani and the extrovert Causio, turns a high percentage of half-chances into goals.

When the Italians get down to their real game it develops as a simple business, with short-passing triangles of players keeping possession in risk-free sorties.

At the back is the nerveless 36-year-old Dino Zoff in goal, with his "protector", the giant Inter-Milan sweeper, Giacinto Facchetti, playing his fourth – and final – World Cup.

But it is in midfield that Bearzot pins all his hopes. Benetti, the Nobby Stiles of the team, the brilliant but inconsistent Antognoni and the Torino star Zaccarelli carry a heavy responsibility – perhaps if Italy fail badly they may even be the cause of the resignation that Bearzot threatened in New York.

Mexico

Colours: Green shirts, white shorts, green stockings.

When Mexico hammered visiting Yugoslavia 5–1 in a friendly match last year it marked what could be a significant breakthrough for the most consistent qualifiers of all the smaller nations. For it suggested that perhaps Mexico are at last equipped to demonstrate that they are worthy of a place in the World Cup Finals as much for their ability as for their luck in being repeatedly presented with an easy passage through the qualifying stages.

Few were surprised to see Mexico's name in the hat when the draw for the Finals was made in Buenos Aires early this year. It was the sixth time in the last seven tournaments that they have survived the qualifying matches. And no wonder, say the cynics, when you consider that their geographical position limits their opposition to no-hopers of the calibre of Guatemala and the United States.

Some of the Mexican squad with their coaching staff. Back row *(from left)*: De La Torre, Gomez, Guillen, Sous, Real, Rexas, Castrejon, Jimenes. Front row: Cuellar, Ranger, Isiordia, Sanchez, Najora

The only real surprise in the last 28 years came when Mexico were denied a place from the Central American zone by Haiti in 1974. Four years earlier, Mexico, as host country, had reached the quarter-finals, heading a Finals group which included Russia and Belgium.

Now team manager Antonio Roca, conveniently glossing over the 1974 setback, believes Mexico can make their biggest-ever impact on the Finals. To underline his confidence he has taken two tremendous gambles – with the team and with his own future. He has liberally sprinkled his team with youngsters like winger Sanchez, 19, strikers Manzo and Zuarza, both 18, and 19-year-old centre-back Martinez. In qualifying matches they have justified their promotion, but the big doubt remains about how their youth, coupled with the traditionally volatile Mexican temperament, will respond to the tremendous tension and pressures in Argentina.

Roca's other bold step came when his own club, Atletico Español, complained that he was devoting too much time to the national team to the detriment of his other role as club manager. Club must come before country, Roca was ordered. He refused to reduce his commitment to the national team – and was sacked by Español. If the Mexican youngsters blow up or freeze in Argentina, Roca's future will look bleak, at national and club level.

Roca appears unconcerned, fortified by the fast, decisive football served up recently by the teenagers, reinforced by more experienced men like midfielders Cuellar and Castrejon. "Everything seems to be in our favour", he says. "The heavy conditions we can expect in the Argentinian winter will be more suited to our style of play, which is more direct than most of the South American countries. And, with the confidence of youth, my players will be going into action in the knowledge that they can match anybody for skill."

To complete his painstaking preparations, Roca takes

his side on a tour of Europe before the Finals. "We want to get to know every style of football so that no one can take us by surprise", he explains.

Peru

Colours: White shirts with red diagonal band, white shorts, white stockings with red tops.

Peru are the old men of the Finals and will field a team that has barely changed from the 1970 tournament. Yes, 1970. Only the recent retirement of Molondez has saved them from the embarrassment of fielding a pair of central defenders whose combined age totals 73. Molondez was 37 when he finally called it a day – but his partner Hector Chumpitaz soldiers on at a sprightly 36.

Chumpitaz, who has won 100 caps, made his international debut in 1964 and was one of Peru's outstanding players in the 1970 tournament when they reached the quarter-finals. A well-built, muscular man, he stands only 5ft 6in and the prospect of him marking Joe Jordan when Peru face Scotland might bring a smile to those north of Hadrian's Wall. Yet Chumpitaz has rarely come out second-best in any heading duel and must never be underrated – even at his advanced age.

Another veteran of the 1970 campaign is the explosive Teofilo Cubillas. He is the pin-up boy of all Peru and scored 35 goals last season to prove that, at 29, his finishing power is not diminishing. After a superbly successful World Cup in Mexico, when he scored a memorable goal in Peru's 3–2 defeat by Brazil, Cubillas joined Basle of Switzerland for £65,000. But he failed to settle and moved to Porto of Portugal, who were then managed by Aymore Moreira, Brazil's World Cup winning manager of 1962. Cubillas stayed two years before returning home in 1976 to join Alianza of Lima.

His clubmate at Lima is the speedy, temperamental Sotil. A winger with a penchant for scoring goals as well,

Speedy Peruvian forward **Hugo Sotil**: his goal-scoring ability is a potential threat to Scotland's chances

Sotil left Peru to join Barcelona. But there he fell out with Johan Cruyff and after a stormy separation he returned to Lima.

Peru's left-winger, Oblitas, also had a spell in Spain. At 26 he is in his prime and will prove a handful for all but the best full-backs. He loves to take on his opponent and possesses a ready eye for the goal chance. The 28-year-old Munante, who will probably be challenging Sotil for his place, is a similar, highly attack-minded player with little idea of defence.

It is this very air of adventure which will prove Peru's greatest weakness. The crowds are sure to love their attractive, flamboyant style of play, full of dummies, long dribbles and spectacular goals. But they are suspect in defence, despite Chumpitaz and their agile, talented goalkeeper Quiroga, a naturalised Argentinian.

They showed what they are capable of in their very tough qualifying group when they beat Chile 2–0, crushed Bolivia 5–0 and then only fell to the highly fancied Brazilians 1–0. The conditions, of course, will be perfect for them, and manager Marcus Calderon – who says he is supremely confident of beating Scotland – has had his squad in a high-altitude training camp since the beginning of March.

Poland

Colours: White shirts, red shorts, red stockings.

Poland lost Sir Alf Ramsey his job and ended Bobby Moore's England career. Moore made one of his rare mistakes, which cost a goal, and at Wembley the Poles weathered the most incredible barrage to end England's hopes of qualifying for the 1974 World Cup. There were ready-made scapegoats for England – Ramsey and Moore. Both went, which, with hindsight, was a bit harsh, for Poland became the team of the tournament, might easily have won in Munich and finished in a highly honourable third place.

Jacek Gmoch has succeeded Gorski, who managed Poland through the glory years that won them the Olympic Championship in 1972 and that third place in Munich two years later. They have not unearthed much new talent and they will be relying heavily on players who

Andrzej Szarmach of Poland: can he reproduce the form he showed in 1974?

took part in the 1974 tournament. That adds up to a lot of experience, and with only West Germany to worry about in their group – Tunisia and Mexico can hardly be real threats – they should not have much trouble in qualifying for the second round.

That is when the real test will come for players like Jan Tomaszewski, the goalkeeper so well remembered for his spectacular acrobatics at Wembley. He was first capped seven years ago as a 22-year-old against West Germany and has now played 56 times for his country. Jerzy Gorgon, the giant central defender, is back in favour after spending two years in the wilderness because he was considered to be overweight and "unresponsive to discipline". Jerzy is again a "probable" along with Henryk Wieczorek, who was in the 1974 World Cup squad; Wladyslaw Zmuda, who although still only 23 has 41 international appearances to his credit; and the promising 19-year-old Roman Wojcicki, who is a near-certainty to gain his first full cap in Argentina.

Kazimierz Deyna, at one time regarded as the best midfield player in Europe, again captains the side. He is the tactician of the team and his record with the national side goes back to the 1972 Olympics. Now 30 years of age, Deyna has collected 92 caps.

Poland will rely heavily on Grzegorz Lato, the right-side striker who was top scorer in Munich with seven goals. He has been capped 60 times and at 27 years of age remains one of Europe's most dangerous wingers.

Newcomers to the squad are midfield players Zbigniew Boniek and Adam Nawalka. Nawalka, aged 20, has made eight appearances for Poland and Boniek, aged 21, has been capped 17 times. Both are highly promising players in the best Polish tradition and are expected to make telling contributions in Argentina.

The attack could be led by 22-year-old Stanislaw Terlecki, centre-forward with LKS Lodz, who has made a formidable impact in the qualifying matches. But almost certain to be included in the forward line is Andrzej Szarmach, who emerged as a star in 1974 and since leaving Gornik Zabrse has now linked up with Lato at Mielec.

Szarmach, now 27 and with 46 caps, and his club

colleague, Lato, could again provide the sparkle in a Polish side that has one serious question to answer: "Are they past their best?"

Scotland

Colours: Dark blue shirts with white trim, white shorts, red stockings.

Scotland will have one huge selection headache when they arrive in Argentina – just who to leave out. Their squad truly bristles with talent, especially in midfield where world-class players like Don Masson, Archie Gemmill, Bruce Rioch, Asa Hartford, Graeme Souness and Lou Macari are battling for positions. Any one of the men ultimately omitted would walk into the England team.

But this is a happy problem for manager Ally MacLeod. His trickiest – and perhaps most vital – decision concerns the goalkeeper. Alan Rough of Partick Thistle has failed to establish himself as the automatic choice and faces stiff competition from Coventry's Jim Blyth. Blyth, a bargain £22,000 buy from Preston back in 1972, has emerged as the dark horse and had an impressive debut when Scotland beat Bulgaria 2–1 at Hampden Park on February 22. Leeds' David Stewart is also useful cover and Ally MacLeod knows all about the other contender, Aberdeen's veteran Bobby Clark. MacLeod was formerly manager at Aberdeen and is a firm admirer of Clark's coolness under pressure. He is the most experienced of the four and a totally efficient, rather than flamboyant, performer.

Whoever gets the final nod will be supported by one of the best defences in Argentina. The only serious question mark hangs over the fitness of Celtic's Danny McGrain, at 27 arguably the finest right-back in the world. A worrying ankle injury has kept him on the sidelines for much of the season, but if he is fit to add to his 40 caps he is a certain starter.

An unfit McGrain would make way for Rangers' Sandy Jardine, who would have almost doubled his 32 international appearances had it not been for his immaculate Celtic rival. Jardine, one of the fastest men in British football, regularly competes on the Scottish professional sprint circuit.

Willie Donachie of Manchester City or Frank Gray of Leeds will play at left-back. Donachie must miss the first match because he has been suspended as a result of two

Danny McGrain: a world-class defender who, if fit, will be an automatic choice for Scotland

Archie Gemmill: one of Scotland's galaxy of midfield stars

bookings collected during the qualifying competition.

The centre of the defence will be dominated by the imposing figure of Gordon McQueen, who cost Manchester United a staggering half a million pounds when they bought him from Leeds. There is unlikely to be a centre-forward to match his mastery in the air – a factor which could also earn Scotland some goals from set pieces. Alongside him should be the equally effective and tigerish Kenny Burns, a revelation since his move from Birmingham to Nottingham Forest and the calming influence of Brian Clough. And, provided he recovers from injury, Manchester United's stylish sweeper Martin

Buchan will be around to pick up any pieces that these two miss.

The midfield will be a contest between Hartford's and Macari's competitiveness; Masson's and Souness's distribution and the tenacity and scoring abilities of Rioch and Gemmill.

Up front Scotland are certain to play with a winger – and once again they are almost spoilt for choice. There is the diminutive but dynamic Arthur Graham of Leeds, the blinding speed of West Brom's Willie Johnston or the all-round control of another Brian Clough/Nottingham Forest success story, John Robertson. Robertson, over-weight and slaphappy before Clough's arrival, emerged as one of the most potent forces in their thrust for the treble.

The man expected to get on the end of the winger's supply of crosses looks likely to be Manchester United's other mammoth signing from Leeds, Joe Jordan. Aston Villa's Andy Gray will push him all the way, though, if he fully recovers from injury. Ian Wallace, Coventry's red-haired little striker, has emerged as a late contender for a supporting role in attack. But one man who can pencil his name in now is Liverpool's Kenny Dalglish.

Dalglish, 26, has won 50 caps and was once described by the legendary Jock Stein as a manager's dream. Since his £440,000 from Celtic to Liverpool to replace Kevin Keegan, Dalglish has been operating mainly as a striker. Before that the little teetotaller had won every honour in the Scottish game as a midfield creator.

Yet even with such an abundance of talent, Scotland's ace could be in the genial shape of manager MacLeod. He has the crucial task of channelling the natural aggression and exuberance of the Scots. Too often in the past their temperament has cost them dear. If MacLeod can convince them of the necessity of turning the other cheek in the face of provocation they have the ability to go all the way.

Spain

Colours: Red shirts, dark blue shorts, black stockings.

Apart from their own team, Spain is the country Argentinians most wanted to qualify for the World Cup Finals. A large percentage of the population have Spanish ancestry and, of course, Spanish is the native tongue. All of this will give Spain a reassuring feeling of acceptance and support among the volatile South Americans and that could prove a vital factor.

They are led by a highly experienced manager in Ladislao Kubala, one of the all-time great players, who appeared for a record three countries – Hungary, Czechoslovakia and Spain. His main problem in blending an international team is that Spain is bulging with highly paid superstar mercenaries – like Cruyff and Neeskens at Barcelona. Rather than develop their own talent, Spanish clubs have always gone out and bought expensively. As a result, many of the finest players in the

Spain's captain Pirri: a skilled and experienced sweeper

Spanish League are ineligible for the national team.

But they have in their skipper, Pirri, a superb sweeper. The 33-year-old Real Madrid star is a classic distributor of the ball in the Danny Blanchflower mould and an alert, intelligent reader of the game. He will need to keep a tight grip on his men because Spain are notoriously bad losers and their temperament will be suspect in the World Cup glare – despite the assured sympathy of the locals.

In front of Pirri will stand the reliable, rock-like Migueli, a 27-year-old central defender from Barcelona. Asensi is their midfield general, the play-maker who will be orchestrating every move, bringing the wingers and central strikers into action. Asensi, 28, from Barcelona, is the key figure in the Spanish team. Manager Kubala will be praying he stays free from injury.

It is in attack that Spain are likely to produce their most memorable contribution to Argentina '78. Apart from the quicksilver Ruben Cano, who scored the winning goal in the vital match with Yugoslavia in Belgrade, Spain have several high-quality strikers who can turn a game with brilliant, individual goals.

Left-winger Cardenosa is a fast, skilful raider who likes to cut inside and attack the goal as well as driving down the flank. And centre-forward Santillana is a truly inspirational figure. The 25-year-old Real Madrid striker was top scorer in the Spanish League last season despite the influx of foreign stars. Only 5ft 10in, he is a whippet-fast operator, much in the style of England's John Richards, with an explosive shot in either foot.

The attack will be supplemented by the experienced, overlapping full-back Comacho, provided he has fully recovered from a recent cartilage operation.

Arconada, in keeping with most Continental goal-keepers, is something of a weak link. He would certainly be struggling to find a place in the English First Division, with his distinct unease when dealing with crosses.

Spain will be determined to make a good show in Argentina – if only because they are scheduled to host the World Cup in 1982.

Sweden

Colours: Yellow shirts, blue shorts, yellow stockings with blue tops.

Sweden have an outstanding record in the World Cup for a nation who have such a lack of interest in the sport that they cannot even support a professional League. Their most successful club side, Malmo, attract gates of only 9–10,000. But even with the majority of the population glued to the ice hockey results rather than the Association Football classified check, Sweden have still managed to reach the World Cup Finals six times.

True, in this last qualifying competition, they had only to beat Switzerland and Norway. But they did so – and they are there while more fashionable nations are not.

Led by manager Georg Ericsson, Sweden will field a living legend in the shape of centre-back Bjorn Nordqvist. The 35-year-old veteran has amassed 106 caps and will surely pass Bobby Moore's all-time record of 108 this summer.

Behind Nordqvist, Sweden have in Holdstroem one of Europe's few world-class goalkeepers outside Great Britain. He had a magnificent World Cup last time in Germany and his form has improved, if anything, to the extent that he is firmly in the running for this year's European Footballer of the Year award.

In midfield, Sweden will revolve around the ball skills and distribution of the highly talented Linderoth, but it will be to their mercurial striker Rald Edstrom that they will look to upset Austria, Spain and Brazil in their group matches. Edstrom, who has been troubled by a series of back injuries, was judged the best centre-forward in the 1974 World Cup Finals by no less an adjudicator

Sweden's star striker Rald Edstrom

than Alfredo di Stefano.

Edstrom spent three highly successful years with PSV Eindhoven in Holland before, surprisingly, returning home to Sweden to join IFK Goteborg last year. The promise of a good, secure job outside football played a major part in the decision.

In only his second game for Sweden, Edstrom headed a hat-trick in a 4–4 draw with Russia. All Sweden will be hoping for a similar performance – provided that suspect back holds out.

Supplementing Edstrom up front will be Sjoberg, a strong, direct striker and Wendt, who was top scorer for Kaiserslautern in the West German Bundesliga last season.

Their service will mainly be supplied by Torstensson, the right-winger who played for Bayern Munich in their European Cup final victory over Leeds. Now with FC Zurich, Torstensson may have lost his devastating edge of pace but he remains a very dangerous player.

Manager Ericsson is not too optimistic about his team's chances. He says: "We have a fine goalkeeper, a fine midfield player in Linderoth and a fine striker in Edstrom. But we lack one brilliant, individual match winner."

Temperamentally, the Swedes are always world-class. But although their tall, tough defence should not concede too many goals nobody can see them emulating their 1974 feat, when they reached the last eight and then fell 4–2 to West Germany after leading 1–0 at half-time.

Tunisia

Colours: Red shirts, white shorts, red stockings.

Tunisia travel to Argentina insisting that they have a significant role to play in the World Cup Finals even though they acknowledge they are unlikely to progress further than the preliminary group matches.

They regard themselves as standard-bearers for the emerging soccer population of Africa – and as living proof that the controversial qualifying zoning system is justified by the way it broadens the appeal and adds dimensions to the overall aspect of soccer.

As England sit it out this summer there will be no shortage of advocates for the argument that a seeding method should be employed to ensure that the 16 strongest nations survive the qualifying matches to contest the Finals. Only in this way, it is contended, will the competition represent a valid assessment of the world soccer table.

Tunisia, naturally, support the counter-argument that the principal object of the World Cup is to encourage the development of the game. And they can rightly claim to be a worthy representative of the emerging soccer nations.

Apart from the senior side's success against teams such as Morocco and Algeria, the spectacular progress of Tunisian soccer was rewarded when their under-18 side

Tunisia's national team. Back row *(from left)*: Gasmi, Agrebi, Kaabi, Temine, Drouib, Attouga. Front row: Tarak, Kamel, Akid, Goummidh, Limam

was invited to compete in the European Junior Championships in Monaco last winter. It was the first time they had competed internationally at this level and, although they won only one of their four matches, their joyful, uninhibited style delighted the fans.

They played fast, open, attacking football, chasing everything, including back-passes from their more defensive-minded opponents that were virtually in the goalkeeper's hands before the Tunisian challenger had set off.

This naive enthusiasm, coupled with excellent ball-control and skilful dribbling, provided considerable entertainment – even if it did founder against the more mature, composed tactics of the Russians, Yugoslavs and Italians.

And, according to Mejid Chetali, manager of Tunisia's World Cup team, the juniors accurately reproduced the style of the senior team. "My players aren't professionals in the normal sense of the word", he explains. "They have full-time jobs and play football more for fun than the part-time wages they collect. As a result their outlook is bound to be rather amateurish. They want to attack all the time. It's quite a job convincing them that it's just as important to establish a sound defence.

"Our experiences in Argentina should take our football a big stride forward. Once my players see at first hand how the top nations secure their foundations my job will be that much easier. At the moment we have the basic skills without the tactical expertise. When that comes we'll be ready to hold our own against the average European countries."

Chetali, a former Tunisian international himself, believes he has several players who could startle opponents in Argentina. "My midfield star Tarak is good enough for any club side in Europe and a number of French teams have been regularly checking him", says Chetali. "We also have a brilliant winger, Temine, who'll be a headache for any full-back. And our most experienced player is our goalkeeper Attouga. He won't let us down."

The Draw

Massive security was mounted for the draw for the Finals at the San Martin Cultural Centre in Buenos Aires on Saturday, January 14. Uniformed and plain-clothes policemen, backed up by troops in combat uniforms with rifles and automatic weapons at the ready, patrolled the passages of the Centre and its surrounding streets.

The nervousness of the Argentinians was easy to understand. With the eyes of the world about to be looking in on them via television it was feared that the Montoneros guerrillas might just fancy intruding on the publicity which the draw was bound to invoke.

The head of the government's World Cup organising committee had been murdered by guerrillas a year earlier on the eve of what would have been his first press conference. Now, with something like 500 foreign journalists assembled with pens poised to record the action, the San Martin Cultural Centre offered itself as an ideal hit spot for the guerrillas.

In fact, the draw went off peacefully, but the guerrilla threat, when the Finals get under way, is still very real – so much so that the Argentinian government has appointed General Juan Carlos Pita to the unenviable position of leading the special World Cup security forces.

The General can claim some intimate knowledge of the guerrillas. He was kidnapped by them a little over a year ago but miraculously escaped and was found wandering down a dirt road in his pyjamas. He was immediately promoted to the rank of General and then put in charge of World Cup security.

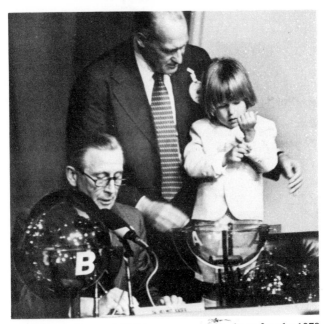

Dr Helmut Kaser of FIFA announces the draw for the 1978 Finals while Ricardo Havelange and his grandfather seem otherwise preoccupied

Let us hope he has a peaceful fortnight, for we want no repetition of the horrifying terrorism that left such dark clouds over the memory of the Munich Olympics.

The World Cup has already attained one landmark. The draw became the first colour television transmission from Argentina, though local viewers still saw it only in black and white. Colour is not expected to be operating inside Argentina until 1981 at the earliest, which is a great pity, because the Argentinians are, by tradition, a colourful people and soccer's most brilliant spectacle loses something of its splendour when it is reproduced in sombre black and white.

However, the fervour for the occasion is by no means diminished and the draw itself was dramatised to the maximum, even to the extent of giving the three-year-old Ricardo Teixeira Havelange, grandson of FIFA president João Havelange, the honour of drawing from a decorated goldfish bowl the names of the nations to make up the four groups.

In fact, there was really little for Ricardo to do, because the big fish had already been designated their spots in the draw. Argentina had been seeded No. 1 in Group One and West Germany as No. 6 in Group Two. Italy were to be No. 4 in Group One, Brazil No. 12 in Group Three and Holland No. 13 in Group Four.

Before little Ricardo's hand was guided into the gold-fish bowl it was also known that Spain, Poland and Scotland would go into Groups Two, Three and Four respectively; Mexico and Peru into Groups Two and Four; Hungary and Sweden into Groups One and Three; with, finally, Iran, Tunisia, Austria and France taking a place in each of the four groups.

So at the end of it all the board read like this:

GROUP ONE
at Buenos Aires and
Mar del Plata

1. **Argentina**

2. **Hungary**

3. **France**

4. **Italy**

GROUP TWO
Buenos Aires, Rosario and
Cordoba

5. **Poland**

6. **West Germany**

7. **Tunisia**

8. **Mexico**

GROUP THREE
Buenos Aires (Velez Sars-
field) and Mar del Plata

9. **Austria**

10. **Spain**

11. **Sweden**

12. **Brazil**

GROUP FOUR
Cordoba, Mendoza

13. **Holland**

14. **Iran**

15. **Peru**

16. **Scotland**

Match Venues

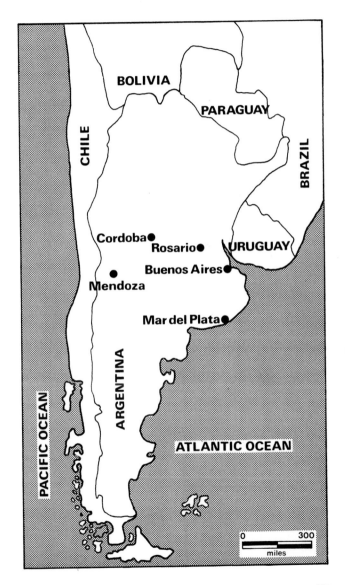

Ally MacLeod, Scotland's manager, was of course delighted. He called the draw "wonderful" and endeared himself greatly to the Argentinian newspapermen, some of whom still smart from the memory of the "animals" tag Sir Alf Ramsey bestowed upon their team in England in 1966.

Ally impressed everyone with his courtesy and his diplomacy and whether or not it was a studied effort in public relations to remove some of the stigma of that 1966 episode we shall never know. But it was certainly a success and Scotland, thanks to Mr MacLeod, are assured a much warmer welcome than ever England might have hoped for.

With two teams to qualify from each group Scotland appear to have a less demanding task in progressing than, say, Italy, who were none too pleased at the prospects confronting them in Group One, where Argentina, with the advantage of playing all their games in Buenos Aires, should be in no great danger. Considerably improved France and the vastly experienced Hungary could well be a problem for the Italians, who, seeded though they were, are in one of the toughest groups.

For the second round the first and second from each group will play in two groups as follows:

GROUP A	GROUP B
Buenos Aires and Cordoba	Rosario and Mendoza
Group One First	Group One Second
Group Two Second	Group Two First
Group Three First	Group Three Second
Group Four Second	Group Four First

The winners of each group will, of course, go on to the final, and the runners-up will play off for third place the day before the final.

When the skirmishes have ended Argentina will have

produced yet more evidence of the fantastic expansion – both in playing the game and watching it – of football all over the globe.

The root cause, of course, is the sheer fascination of the ball, which has a magnetic appeal to every child, whatever his creed or colour. But the real disciples were the British colonialists, the civil servants and the English, Scottish, Irish and Welsh soldiers, who took a football with them wherever they travelled.

For the emergent nations, awakening to independence after years of foreign subjection, football offers a foundation on which to base their nationalistic feelings and assert themselves at international level.

Football is now *the* universal game, a sport with which every nation and every nation's population can instantly identify.

That is why getting to Argentina was so important and doing well there is even more so.

Televising the World Cup

It is something of a tribute to the know-how of British television that the 38 member nations of the European Broadcasting Union elected Cornishman Bill Ward as head of European Broadcasts, incorporating TV and radio, for the World Cup.

Bill, who started with the BBC in 1936 and then moved to ITV in 1959, has been in the game a little longer than anyone else and he started his fact-finding missions in Argentina in 1976. Since then he has been back five times (it is a 19-hour flight from London to Buenos Aires) to complete the preparations that will give live action to a world audience in excess of 600 million. Thirty European nations, 10 Iron Curtain countries, 10 South American and 15 Far East and Middle East states will be taking live transmissions.

The Argentinians will man the 48 cameras involved in the coverage. To ensure they are *au fait* with world requirements Bill Ward organised a two-week seminar in Germany last year where the acknowledged top soccer producers – like BBC's Alec Weeks – lectured on techniques.

The Argentinian camera crews were also given practical experience, covering West German football matches. The style and pattern of coverage is based absolutely on what we have come to expect from Wembley – acknowledged to be the best in the world – and the cost to the Argentinians has been astronomic.

They have built three new stadiums and rebuilt three more at a cost of over £225 million, of which, in ad-

The River Plate Stadium in Buenos Aires, from where the opening match will be televised on June 1

vertising and advance ticket sales, they have already recouped something approaching £40 million. The balance will never be made good, but the Argentinians will be left with a brand new communications system, comprising telephones, telex, radio and an up-to-the-minute television production centre that will have cleared all the obstacles in the way of domestic colour TV by 1981.

They will also be left with the most modern soccer stadiums in the world, with segregated areas for newspapermen accessible by entrances sometimes a mile from the ground and passing the special practice areas where the World Cup finalists will have their pre-match warm-up sessions.

Argentina is taking this opportunity to show itself off and, with the advice of such as Bill Ward, has skimped nothing to present a pleasing picture.

The 1978 Results

Times of matches given in this section are local times: to convert to British time, add on four hours.

FIRST ROUND/**Fixtures and Results**

June 1/15.00/Buenos Aires   GROUP TWO

West Germany   *v.*   **Poland**
Scorers: *Scorers:*
....
.... (..........) (..........) ....
....
....

June 2/19.15/Buenos Aires   GROUP ONE

Hungary   *v.*   **Argentina**
Scorers: *Scorers:*
....
.... (..........) (..........) ....
....
....

June 2/13.45/Mar del Plata   GROUP ONE

France   *v.*   **Italy**
Scorers: *Scorers:*
....
.... (..........) (..........) ....
....
....

June 2/16.45/Rosario   GROUP TWO

Tunisia   *v.*   **Mexico**
Scorers: *Scorers:*
....
.... (..........) (..........) ....
....
....

June 3/13.45/Buenos Aires (V.S.) **GROUP THREE**

Spain   *v.*   **Austria**
Scorers: *Scorers:*

....
.... (............) (............) ....
....
....

June 3/13.45/Mar del Plata   **GROUP THREE**

Sweden   *v.*   **Brazil**
Scorers: *Scorers:*

....
.... (............) (............) ....
....
....

June 3/16.45/Cordoba   **GROUP FOUR**

Peru   *v.*   **Scotland**
Scorers: *Scorers:*

....
.... (............) (............) ....
....
....

June 3/16.45/Mendoza   **GROUP FOUR**

Iran   *v.*   **Holland**
Scorers: *Scorers:*

....
.... (............) (............) ....
....
....

June 6/19.15/Buenos Aires   **GROUP ONE**

Argentina   *v.*   **France**
Scorers: *Scorers:*

....
.... (............) (............) ....
....
....

June 6/13.45/Mar del Plata   GROUP ONE

Italy   *v.*   **Hungary**
Scorers: *Scorers:*

....
.... (..........) (..........) ....
                                               ....
                                               ....

June 6/16.45/Rosario   GROUP TWO

Poland   *v.*   **Tunisia**
Scorers: *Scorers:*

....
.... (..........) (..........) ....
                                               ....
                                               ....

June 6/16.45/Cordoba   GROUP TWO

Mexico   *v.*   **West Germany**
Scorers: *Scorers:*

....
.... (..........) (..........) ....
                                               ....
                                               ....

June 7/13.45/Buenos Aires (V.S.)   GROUP THREE

Austria   *v.*   **Sweden**
Scorers: *Scorers:*

....
.... (..........) (..........) ....
                                               ....
                                               ....

June 7/13.45/Mar del Plata   GROUP THREE

Brazil   *v.*   **Spain**
Scorers: *Scorers:*

....
.... (..........) (..........) ....
                                               ....
                                               ....

June 7/16.45/Cordoba

Scotland *v.* **Iran**

Scorers: *Scorers:*

....
.... (.........) (.........) ....
....
....

June 7/16.45/Mendoza

Holland *v.* **Peru**

Scorers: *Scorers:*

....
.... (.........) (.........) ....
....
....

June 10/19.15/Buenos Aires

Italy *v.* **Argentina**

Scorers: *Scorers:*

....
.... (.........) (.........) ....
....
....

June 10/13.45/Mar del Plata

France *v.* **Hungary**

Scorers: *Scorers:*

....
.... (.........) (.........) ....
....
....

June 10/16.45/Rosario

Mexico *v.* **Poland**

Scorers: *Scorers:*

....
.... (.........) (.........) ....
....
....

June 10/16.45/Cordoba GROUP TWO

Tunisia *v.* **West Germany**

Scorers: *Scorers:*

.... (..........) (..........) ....
....
....

June 11/13.45/Buenos Aires (V.S.) GROUP THREE

Sweden *v.* **Spain**

Scorers: *Scorers:*

.... (..........) (..........) ....
....
....

June 11/13.45/Mar del Plata GROUP THREE

Brazil *v.* **Austria**

Scorers: *Scorers:*

.... (..........) (..........) ....
....
....

June 11/16.45/Cordoba GROUP FOUR

Peru *v.* **Iran**

Scorers: *Scorers:*

.... (..........) (..........) ....
....
....

June 11/16.45/Mendoza GROUP FOUR

Scotland *v.* **Holland**

Scorers: *Scorers:*

.... (..........) (..........) ....
....
....

SCOTLAND'S TEAMS IN THE FIRST ROUND, GROUP FOUR

v. **Peru**

No	Name
	Substitutions

Scorers:

....
....
....
....

v. **Iran**

No	Name
	Substitutions

Scorers:

....
....
....
....

v. **Holland**

No	Name
	Substitutions

Scorers:

....
....
....
....

FIRST ROUND/**Final Results**

Group One	P	W	D	L	F	A	Pts
1							
2							
3							
4							

Winner...(goes through to Group A)
Second ....(goes through to Group B)

Group Two	P	W	D	L	F	A	Pts
1							
2							
3							
4							

Winner...(goes through to Group B)
Second ....(goes through to Group A)

Group Three

		P	W	D	L	F	A	Pts
1								
2								
3								
4								

Winner...(goes through to Group A)
Second ....(goes through to Group B)

Group Four

		P	W	D	L	F	A	Pts
1								
2								
3								
4								

Winner...(goes through to Group B)
Second ....(goes through to Group A)

SECOND ROUND/Fixtures and Results

June 14/13.45/Buenos Aires   GROUP A

  Group Two Second   *v.*   Group One First

....
Scorers: (..........) (..........) *Scorers:*
....
....
....
....

June 14/13.45/Cordoba   GROUP A

  Group Three First   *v.*   Group Four Second

....
Scorers: (..........) (..........) *Scorers:*
....
....
....
....

June 14/16.45/Rosario   **GROUP B**

    Group Two First   *v.*   Group One Second

    .... (............) (............) ....

    Scorers: *Scorers:*

    ....

    ....

    ....

    ....

June 14/16.45/Mendoza   **GROUP B**

    Group Three Second   *v.*   Group Four First

    .... (............) (............) ....

    Scorers: *Scorers:*

    ....

    ....

    ....

    ....

June 18/16.45/Buenos Aires   **GROUP A**

    Group One First   *v.*   Group Three First

    .... (............) (............) ....

    Scorers: *Scorers:*

    ....

    ....

    ....

    ....

June 18/16.45/Cordoba   **GROUP A**

    Group Four Second   *v.*   Group Two Second

    .... (............) (............) ....

    Scorers: *Scorers:*

    ....

    ....

    ....

    ....

June 18/13.45/Rosario   GROUP B

Group One Second   *v.*   Group Three Second

Scorers: (..........) (..........) *Scorers:*

June 18/13.45/Mendoza   GROUP B

Group Four First   *v.*   Group Two First

Scorers: (..........) (..........) *Scorers:*

June 21/13.45/Buenos Aires   GROUP A

Group Four Second   *v.*   Group One First

Scorers: (..........) (..........) *Scorers:*

June 21/13.45/Cordoba   GROUP A

Group Three First   *v.*   Group Two Second

Scorers: (..........) (..........) *Scorers:*

June 21/16.45/Rosario   **GROUP B**

Group Four First   *v.*   Group One Second

....
Scorers: (............) (............) *Scorers:*
....
....
....
....

June 21/16.45/Mendoza   **GROUP B**

Group Three Second   *v.*   Group Two First

....
Scorers: (............) (............) *Scorers:*
....
....
....
....

SCOTLAND'S TEAMS IN THE SECOND ROUND

v............................. *v.*............................ *v.*............................

No	Name		No	Name		No	Name
	Substitutions			Substitutions			Substitutions

Scorers: *Scorers:*   *Scorers:*
....
....
....
....

SECOND ROUND/**Final Results**

Group A

		P	W	D	L	F	A	Pts
1								
2								
3								
4								

Winner..(goes through to the Final)
Second ....(goes through to Third Place
Play-off)

Group B

		P	W	D	L	F	A	Pts
1								
2								
3								
4								

Winner..(goes through to the Final)
Second ....(goes through to Third Place
Play-off)

Third Place Play-off
June 24/15.00/Buenos Aires

.... *v.* ....

Half time ....
Full time ....
Extra time ....

No	Name
	Substitutions

No	Name
	Substitutions

Scorers:

....
....
....
....

Scorers:

....
....
....
....

Nick *Pts*
Hn 812586 - Home
- Work - Fax 235576.
Lane
Fareham.

The Final
June 25/15.00/Buenos Aires

.... *v.* ....

EGREMONT Half time ....
Full time ....
Extra time ....

No	Name
	Substitutions

No	Name
	Substitutions

Scorers:

....
....
....
....

Scorers:

....
....
....
....

World Cup Winners 1978 ....